72 Hours Gross Darkness

Prepare!

Copyright

October 9, 2023, by G J H

Bibliography

Dederen, R: Gugliotto, L, J: Noris, D, T: Horn, S, H:Nichole, F, D (2019). The Seventh-day Adventist Bible Commentary Vols. 1-7. Review and Herald Publishing Association.

GoForth Parnell, V. {Vicky GoForth Parnell}. (2022, May 06) Another Pesttilence Coming Dream 5/6-2022 @ 6:58 am [Video] Rumble.

GoForth Parnell, V. {Vicky GoForth Parnell}. (2023, May 10) The 3 Days of Darkness is at Hand 5-20-23 @ 11:23 am [Video]. You Tube.

Houteff, V.T. (1990). The Shepherd's Rod. General *Association of Davidian Seventh Day Adventist.*

Peterson, S. {Stephen Peterson}. (2023, September 30) 2nd Exodus: "The Birthing" #2nd Exodus #Qam Yasharahla [Video]. You Tube.

Peterson, S. {Stephen Peterson}. (2023, October 27) 3 Days of Darkness: "The Revelation" Part 1 [Video]. You Tube.

Ready, U B {UB Ready}. (2023, August 9) PROPHECY -- DARKNESS APPROACHING [Video]. You Tube.

Ready, U B {UB Ready}. (2018, August 8) VISION-- DARK MATTER [Video]. You Tube.

Regina, Harvest-Min (2023, June 21) Darkness is Coming Be Ready/#Communion [Video]. You Tube.

Vlaming, S {Sabine Vlaming}. (2023, Jun 18) The Three Days of Darkness and the Second Exodus| Part 1 of 2 [Video]. You Tube.

Table of Content

SECTION ONE

SECTION TWO

SECTION THREE

SECTION FOUR

PREFACE

I am sure it is no secret to anyone, that we are living in the last days, and that Yahushua HaMashiach is coming back, most likely sooner than we think. All things considered; we must expect that some out of the ordinary events will continue to happen. They will take place in rapid and quick succession. One such event is the much talked about topic of the expected "**Three Days and Nights of Darkness**." But even though there is a continuous chatter about this, so many, too many people are still oblivious to it. I try to bring this topic up to the people around me whether I know them or not, for by so doing, I can help them to prepare for this inevitable occurrence soon to come. In all honesty, in most cases I feel ignored. I get the impression that people either do not care, or maybe they think that if they dismiss what I am saying to them, this upcoming event will just go away. Maybe it would not happen. Well, let me say this, regardless of how you feel, it will happen! This event is coming to an unassuming world, and you must get ready for it. So, to all who have already heard about these Three Days and Nights of Darkness, and have done nothing to prepare, **BEGIN TO PREPARE NOW!** And to all those who are hearing about it for the first time, **BEGIN TO PREPARE NOW!** Time is running out, and this event is soon to happen. You don't have a choice in the matter. As it approaches us, what we must do whether we like it or not is to **PREPARE!**

INTRODUCTION

You might be asking yourself the question as to whether this will be the first time for darkness to cover the earth. Good question, one that will be answered as I get deeper into the script. What I can say is that knowing what happened in the past cannot help you if you are not prepared to intelligently face the future. Just know that this is not a situation subject to just one or two countries. This is a situation that the whole world will experience at the same time, without exception and without fail. My main concern is that, yet another person would know what is coming, based on the information given here, but would do nothing to help both themselves and others to be safe at this time. Don't let this be you. The Most High help those who help themselves! This darkness will take most people by surprise. But to those who read and take heed, blessed are you. And now it's time to get into the nitty gritty of this much avoided topic of the Three Days and Nights of Darkness and how to prepare for it. Please look at all videos in the bibliography, for there is where most of this information comes from. All Bible text are taken from the King James Version (KJV). Now, let us begin.

Oh World in Darkness

SECTION ONE
Past Biblical Occurrences

Have you ever watched the movie The Ten Commandments? Well, if you are not yet aware; that movie, even though not one hundred percent accurately depicted, is a true Biblical story. And if you have not yet read that story, it would behoove you to remove the dust from off your Bible, go to the book of Exodus and read it. If you do not have a Bible, then by all means, take a trip to the store and get yourself a King James Version, and please do not use the excuse that you have no money because some Dollar stores carry them for just one dollar and twenty-five cents ($1.25). But if you would not read for yourselves, I will give you the Exodus account here, with particular interest to the plague of three days of darkness, at no extra cost. And it reads: - And the LORD said unto Moses, Stretch out thine hand toward heaven, that there may be darkness over the land of Egypt, even darkness which may be felt. And Moses stretched forth his hand toward heaven; and there was a thick darkness in all the land of Egypt three days: They saw not one another, neither rose any from his place for three days: but all the children of Israel had light in their dwellings. And Pharaoh called unto Moses, and said, Go ye, serve the LORD; only let your flocks and your herds be stayed: let your little ones also go with you. And Moses said, Thou must give us also sacrifices and burnt offerings, that we may sacrifice unto the LORD our God. Our cattle also shall go with us; there shall not an hoof be left behind; for thereof must we take to serve the LORD our God; and we know not with what we must serve the LORD, until we come thither. But the LORD hardened Pharaoh's heart, and he would not let them go. And Pharaoh said unto him, Get thee from me, take heed to thyself, see my face no more; for in that day thou seest my face thou shalt die. And Moses said, Thou hast spoken well, I will see thy face again no more Exodus 10:21-29 KJV. This was not the only plague Yahuveh sent against Pharaoh and the Egyptians. It was the ninth plague, but during this one, Pharoah got so terrified that when the sun came back out, he called Moses and told him "Go ye, serve the LORD." Yes, his heart was still hardened against Yahuveh, but fear caused him to utter words that he did not truly mean, nor was he willing to execute.

Note here, that what came with darkness was terror, of which other future Biblical instances were prophesied of also. Another such occurrence happened, though for a shorter period, but bringing to prominence the number three, was the crucifixion of Yahushua HaMashiach. The account states that "from the sixth hour there was darkness over all the land unto the ninth hour. And about the ninth hour Jesus cried with a loud voice, saying, Eli, Eli, lama sabachthani…………….. Some of them that stood there, when they heard that, said, This man calleth for Elias. And straightway one of them ran, and took a spunge, and filled it with vinegar, and put it on a reed, and gave him to drink. The rest said, Let be, let us see whether Elias will come to save him. Jesus, when he had cried again with a loud voice, yielded up the ghost. And, behold, the veil of the temple was rent in twain from the top to the bottom; and the earth did quake, and the rocks rent; And the graves were opened; and many bodies of the saints which slept arose, And came out of the graves after his resurrection, and went into the holy city, and appeared unto many." Mathew 27:45-53 KJV. See here also that this

Darkness fell from the sixth to the ninth hour.

darkness brought the terror of an earthquake, along with rented rocks, the veil of the temple being rented in twain from the top to the bottom, open graves, and a resurrection. So, what I am noticing here is that this type of gross darkness prompts significant events in the history of the earth. In Pharaoh's time, it was the Exodus of Israel out of Egypt, and in Yahushua's time, it was the bringing to conclusion the sacrificial system, because the veil of the temple tore in two, notwithstanding the terror of earthquake and open graves. Do you think things would be any different in our time? As a matter of fact, from what I understand, events would be way worse.

There is Nothing New Under the Sun

"And it shall come to pass in that day, saith the Lord God, that I will cause the sun to go down at noon, and I will darken the earth in the clear day," Amos 8:9 KJV.

This is what is up ahead of us. You will not be in your cozy comfortable bed when this happens. You will be up and about at high noon. Question: Can you think about some of the thing people worldwide do at noon? Here are some of the things that people might be found doing at midday: - How about flying in an airplane filled with passengers. Can you think about what would happen to that airplane?

Or maybe on a cruise ship filled with passengers. Can you imagine what would happen to that cruise ship?

What about being stuck on a busy highway in midday traffic. What happens to all those speeding vehicles with huge trucks bearing down on either side of them, with no one able to see who is next to them or what they must do or where they must go next.

But there are other major issues to consider here. You might be at work, or at the supermarket, the movies, or the laundry mat. You must stay there and not look out into the darkness.

Your children might be at school, and you have no way to reach them, or family members are not together and unable to get home. Begin to speak to your children and the rest of your family, devising a plan as to how to deal with the darkness from now on.

These are some of the things expected to happen when sudden darkness falls, and it is pitch-black outside, in the face of unprepared confused people, unable to navigate themselves in unfamiliar darkness. And for this reason. It is paramount to begin to prepare for this event.

The Reason for Seventy-Two Hours of Darkness

When it was time for Israel to make their exodus out of Egypt, this event was preceded by ten plagues namely: - Water turned to blood, Plague of frogs, Plague of lice or gnats, Plague of flies, Plague of pestilence killing livestock, Plague of boils, Plague of hail, Plague of locust, Plague of darkness, and Plague of the death of the firstborn commonly known as the Passover. These were judgments, with seventy-two hours of darkness being plague number nine. In like manner, when it's time for Yahushua HaMashiach to gather His people out from The United States of America and from among the other nations, He brings judgements upon the earth that would cause people to repent thus, purifying them and strengthening their faith in Him. These ten plagues will fall again, only this time upon the entire sinful world and in a different sequence, but the plague of darkness will happen again right before the exodus occurs. This gathering of the people from among the nations is called the

Second Exodus.

Three Group of People Involved

All People will be impacted by this event, but not in the same way. The three groups involved are 1- The Faithful 2-The Lukewarm and 3- The Unsaved.

<u>The first group</u> of faithful believers know what to do at that time. They will be supernaturally protected and provided for while abiding in Yahushua. "That He might present it to *himself a glorious church*, not having spot, or wrinkle, or any such thing; but that it should be holy and without blemish." Ephesians 5:27 KJV. They are the prepared ones, who heed the warning sign and go indoors, cover their windows, and close all doors. They will have electric light in their dwellings which can be supernatural light. And a way of escape will be made for them before the beginning of the Great Tribulation. Isaiah 60:1, 2 KJV says, "Arise, shine; for thy light is come, and the glory of the LORD is risen upon thee. For, behold, the darkness shall cover the earth, and gross darkness the people: but the LORD shall arise upon thee, and his glory shall be seen upon thee." These are the wise virgins with oil in their lamps whose light has not gone out. These people

Faithful Saints with Unspotted Garments.

will literally light up in their bodies. Therefore, "Let thy garments be always white; and let thy head lack no ointment," Ecclesiastes 9:8 KJV.

Children and feeble-minded people worldwide will also be supernaturally protected. They are expected to be taken to heavenly safety at the onset of this falling darkness. The sudden snatching away of children causes some unaware parents to become distraught, not knowing what happened to their children. "Thus saith the LORD; A voice was heard in Ramah, lamentation, and bitter weeping; Rachel weeping for her children refused to be comforted for her children, because they were not," Jeremiah 31:15 KJV. But instead of weeping, they should take comfort in this, because their precious little ones will be eternally protected from then on.

The second group of believers are Laodicean in nature. They are lukewarm and pharisaic with spots on their garments. But although they are lacking in faith, love, and obedience, they will still have a measure of spiritual protection. They will use candles, oil lamps or whatever other form of light they have on hand to light their houses and will at this time be given a chance to cry out to Yahuveh in repentance. As they submit themselves to Him, in all spiritual areas, they will be safeguarded from demonic forces roaming outside. But if they remain indoors with their doors and windows closed until the darkness is fully lifted, while prayerfully seeking The Father in childlike trust and obedience, He will deliver them during this most horrific time.

<u>The third group</u> of people are the unsaved. These are those who have rejected Yahushua HaMashiach. They are disobedient, rebellious, and sinful in nature. Therefore, at this time, their homes will be engulfed in an oppressive darkness both spiritually and physically. They will also be pursued by demonic forces wanting to enter their dark homes without having any form of light. And if through ignorance of the dangers facing them in this situation, they attempt to venture outside for any reason, they would become possessed and devoured by demonic forces seeking to harm them. On the other hand, if they wholeheartedly repent and turn to Yahuveh and His Son in trust and obedience, He will lift them up and save them.

Laodicean Spirit Accusing the Brethren.

A Personal Visitation

Hence, the lukewarm and the unsaved will be granted a personal visitation by the Most High who gives them a chance to repent and be saved, like what He did with Jonah in the belly of the fish, and with Paul on the road to Damascus. Isaiah 9:2 KJV says, "The people that walked in darkness have seen a great light: they that dwell in the land of the shadow of death, upon them hath the light shinned." But if these people remain hard-hearted and refuse to repent, a time of great sorrow and unprecedented trials and tribulations will follow, to severely discipline and chastise them. When Yahushua HaMashiach was seen after "heaven opened, and behold a white horse; and he that sat upon him was called Faithful and True, and in righteousness he doth judge and make war," Revelation 19:11 KJV. He makes war with the unsaved who refused to accept Him and be saved.

*** Some of the above Revelations are found on You Tube video by Sabine Vlaming, entitled "The Three Days of Darkness and the Second Exodus| Part 1 of 2."

Jonah spent three days in the belly of the fish after trying to run away from Yahuwah, and Paul was blind for three days after his Damascus Road encounter. They both experienced three days and nights of Darkness.

Vicky GoForth Parnell

Hear what Yahuveh's watchman; Vicky GoForth Parnell was told about these seventy-two hours. "The time of the time of the Three Days of Darkness is at hand daughter. I move my hand upon this world, darkness comes. The time is upon you O world; a time of darkness that has never been felt since Pharoh's days of old. Darkness that is alive; darkness that penetrates the very soul of the wicked evil hearted people. This is the outer darkness of hell that is descending upon your world by my command. There will be weeping and gnashing of teeth as madness sets into the minds of the rebellious, stiff-necked, self-willed, evil people of your world. This is judgement for your sins. This is mercy inside of my righteous judgement because your sins are worthy of death. In the darkness during these three days, every man woman and child of the age of understanding right from wrong, will by divine means for some, be given a chance to repent for your wicked evil doings. "What evil do we do that would cause a God of love to do this to us? You are supposed to be a God of love," I hear before even the darkness comes. I AM righteous, holy, pure, and my judgements are

15

unbiased, unlike man's whose thinking are corrupted by sin. You have sinned against your holy God and creator. You have sinned against each other. You have sinned against your own bodies. The days of darkness is a time for all to repent. It is a time for the wicked to be judged. I AM the righteous judge! My standards are not yours but Heaven's, and you would go through these three days of darkness O world whether you call me Savior of this world or not. Whether you acknowledge my Father in Heaven as God or not. We are who we are regardless of your futile words and mindless beliefs. It is out of love for the lost still to come in addition to the judgements for the wicked, to begin in full force and not in partial increments. I take my Bride who will not have to endure fully the total three days if their hearts are truly ready. Repentance can still be found inside the darkness to come. Those who are my bride made ready, spotless white in me; in my very own righteousness, I say, I come for you. But until this time in the three days of darkness, you would be blessed with the supernatural ability through me to have electric powers supplied to your homes. This is my favor

I am giving to you my dear children, my bride, who is eagerly waiting for my return.

Again I say, if the darkness descends and you have no power of any kind, no light except candle light, then you of my children have been found with sin in your lives. Fall on your knees and repent immediately, for I come quickly for mine. For those who are ready for my return, there is no straddling the fence. Children who call me their Savior and Lord. I say this is not acceptable. I am not coming back for a dirty bride. Who do you love more, the world or me? You know in your hearts as I do, so repent now.

For those who find they are in total darkness, you belong to Satan. You will hear the demons screaming in the darkness. But if you remain inside, you will only have to deal with the tormenting darkness that runs through your soul, causing stark terror as your world calls it. Many hearts shall fail during this time of darkness. My children straddling the fence, loving their sin, who have been disobedient to my cries to clean your temple, your lives up, you too shall hear the sounds of the evil demons and spirits outside, who have been released to fulfil the remaining days of tribulation foretold in my Scripture of Truth; my Word which is Me. I am Jesus Christ. I AM the Son of the one true living God Jehovah. All who are caught out in the open who do not belong of evil spiritual nature shall be torn apart by the evil spirits and powers released in their rage of having finally been released for many from their holy imprisonment. If you are caught outside as my auroras descend over your whole world, seek shelter immediately. Little children of mine, this is one of your Isaiah 26:20-21 moments. As the darkness begins its descent at the end of the auroras of dancing lights upon your whole world, the sun will begin darkening. It would be but a mere moment of time. Make your preparations now oh foolish sleepers of mine. I warn you this last time through this daughter of mine. If you have lights, you have all your access to all your abilities to provide food for those in your homes. If you have prepared and bought what's needed in advance. I shall speak to all of my children's families whether it be one member or twenty. This is if you seek me and ask of me. Remember oh my children, both obedient and disobedient, if you are not sure of the condition of your hearts, then prepare to have food not needing preparations unless you have other means in which I have led you to prepare for.

The time of the three days of darkness is in my hands, and no other. Even in the darkness, only my father knows when He sends me after my own. Oh world created by our hands, your time of darkness has come, has come, has come. Run into me my children, my little ones who truly love me, and I shall hide you as this indignation falls heavy upon your world, the people above and below, every part of what I have created. I do my Father's bidding, and it is just. "**For I came down from heaven, not to do mine own** will, but the will of him that sent me," John 6:38 JKV

SECTION TWO

CERN

Question: What is CERN?
Answer: CERN is a stargate portal into other realms.

 19

This European Organization for Nuclear Research uses the largest **Hadron Collider** for particle acceleration. Their physicists and engineers study those fundamental particles that are the building blocks of the universe. CERN is located in a northwestern suburb of Geneva, on the France–Switzerland border.

What Causes Such Darkness

A Prophecy and Prophetic Vision

These can be found on the You Tube channel "U B Ready."

The Prophecy: August 9th, 2023. The Lord titled this Word "Darkness Approaches," and the scripture He gave was Luke 21: 34-36 KJV which reads, "And take heed to yourselves, lest at any time your hearts be overcharged with surfeiting, and drunkenness, and cares of this life, and so that day come upon you unawares. For as a snare shall it come on all them that dwell on the face of the whole earth. Watch ye therefore, and pray always, that ye may be accounted worthy to escape all these things that shall come to pass, and to stand before the Son of man." And this is the Word. "My son, hear and write these words to warn my children that darkness approaches. This darkness is unlike anything ever seen on earth in modern times. This darkness is thick and has life. It moves and covers the earth, and all that enter it will be crushed by the pressure of evil. Within this darkness death is king. This darkness once fell upon Egypt and took the first born, but this darkness I speak of now will take all who are out in it. My son, tell my children to trust in me. As I have kept the children of Israel safe during that darkness, I will keep those I have marked safe during this darkness. Many will be caught unaware as the darkness approaches, and evil within will overwhelm them. This darkness is the demonic forces that have been loosed during this period of the tribulation. They will consume all who walk in the darkness. This darkness will appear as thick black smoke or fog and will cover the entire earth. My son, this darkness come from man wanting to open portals into other dimensions, but instead, open the gates of hell to lose upon the world great evil. Those in my body that have seen CERN have seen correctly. This technology is from fallen angels who seek nothing more than to destroy all my creation. Beware of false prophets who speak lies to lead my children away from the truth, just as Hananiah spoke lies to lead the children of Judah away from the truth.

Many have fallen for the lies speaking of greatness to come. I say, darkness approaches. My son, continue to warn my children and tell them to prepare, for darkness approaches. Shout repent now. Have your lamps full and your wicks trimmed. This judgement of darkness is to wake up my children out of their sleeping and to seek me in prayer. During this darkness I will visit my remnant and prepare them for what lies ahead. Seek me in all things and stay on your knees in prayer, darkness approaches, but I am the light that dispels the darkness. AMEN! Lord Jesus"

<u>The Prophetic Vision</u>: given on August 8th, 2018 and recorded August 13th, 2023. The Lord titled this vision "Dark Matter." The scripture He gave was Habakkuk 2:1-3 KJV which reads, "I will stand upon my watch, and set me upon the tower, and will watch to see what he will say unto me, and what I shall answer when I am reproved. And the LORD answered me, and said, Write the vision, and make it plain upon tables, that he may run that readeth it. For the vision is yet for an appointed time, but at the end it shall speak, and

not lie: though it tarry, wait for it; because it will surely come, it will not tarry." On that date the Lord spoke to me the words, "Dark Matter." At first I thought, "what was that? Dark Matter." I continued to pray, but the Lord then repeated it several more times, and I thought," Lord, why are you telling me this?" Again, I continued on praying, but after He repeated it a few more times I felt to stop praying and listen to what He wanted to tell me. I sat down with my Bible and was drawn to the scriptures listed above. I then asked the Lord if this is where He wanted me to read. And He replied, "yes, Dark Matter." As soon as He said that I was instantly drawn into an open eye vision, and taken into a location, where I found myself standing directly in front of the statue of the Goddess Sheba that is in front of the CERN facility. I felt the presence of the Lord to my side, and I asked Him, "What am I doing here?" He then asked me, "What do you see?" I said, "I see a false God named Sheba." The Lord said to me, "What does it represent?" Not being a hundred percent sure I said, "I think it represents chaos and destruction." He said, "My son, you are correct. In a very short time from now, America will live this." I understand this to mean that America will soon be living in chaos and destruction. I then asked the Lord, "What about Dark Matter, I understand America will live chaos and destruction so why are you saying Dark Matter?" Upon asking that, I was immediately taken into the CERN building and the Lord and I were standing at the back of a large room, that looked like some type of laboratory. Directly in front of me on the other side of the room, I could see a man from the back. He was standing and facing some type of glassed in area. He had on a white lab coat, and his hands were inside of gloves that were inserted through the glass into this area. It looked like one of those precaution areas that are used to keep from getting exposure to some dangerous substance. Then the Lord brought me closer to the man so I could get a better view and observe what he was doing. I found myself standing just to the side and slightly behind the man and was able to see through the glass wall and watch him while he was working. I saw many tiny silver-colored vials in rows in a container on the counter inside the glass. They look to be about one inch high and a half inch in diameter. The man was using extreme caution as he worked. He used mechanical fingers to pick up one vial at a time and then slowly place it in a small box. He then closed and sealed the lid on the box and then slowly brought it out through the glass area and carefully placed it on the table beside him. I watched him do this a couple of times. Then, with the next box, as he was pulling it through the glass, the lid accidentally got caught and popped open. With that, the vial flew out of the box, hit the floor, and broke. Immediately, and I mean MMEDIATELY, the room filled with darkness. So dark and so fast, that I could not see a thing. I can only say it was almost like the darkness exploded into the room and filled the entire room in the fraction of a second. I could not see a thing. It was total pitch-black darkness. The next thing I knew, we were outside of the CERN building, and I saw the darkness fly out of the building and begin to expand out in every direction. The more it spread, the faster it seemed to go covering more and more. The Lord then said, "Dark matter will cover the world for three days. The people in this building will be responsible for unleashing Dark Matter. They are collecting it to use as a weapon. A drop of Dark Matter escapes, and the world is plunged into darkness. During this time, portals will be opened, and unimaginable things will be loosed upon man." The Lord then brought me up above the building as I watched the bellowing darkness

25

rapidly expand out exponentially, like a thick black non-transparent fog or smoke all across the land. He took me up very high to where I had a view of the whole earth. I watched as the darkness spread so quickly, going out in every direction until it covered the whole world in what appeared to me like just a matter of minutes. As the vision was ending, the Lord showed me a man's face in the distance. As I continued to watch, his face was brought closer and closer and got larger and clearer. When his face was close to me, I saw that this man had a grey beard, longer greyish hair and had on a lab coat. There was a look of horror on his face with his eyes wide open as if he was screaming out in terror. He looked like a scientist and reminded me somewhat of Albert Einstein. I got the sense that this man was the scientist responsible for the incident. The vision ended. The Lord then spoke these words to me, "My son, I have showed you this to prepare the people; to prepare my remnant. The dark matter will diffuse in three days. The light will return to the earth. NOTHING WILL BE THE SAME EVER AGAIN! I AM COMING SOON - THROUGH THE DARK MATTER. BE READY MY REMNANT!" AMEN! Lord Jesus.

SECTION THREE

The Northern Lights Aurora Borealis

The Sign that the Three Days of Darkness are Here.

The Sign that the Three Days of Darkness are Here.

Question: What is the Aurora Borealis?

Answer: The northern lights, also known as the aurora borealis, are a beautiful natural display of dancing waves of light, predominantly seen in high latitude regions. The lights appear as rays, spirals, or dynamic flickers covering the entire sky.

Here are what some messengers of the Lord said about these warning signs, as a heads up to get into your houses immediately before this big event occurs. I am summarizing.

"The aurora lights in the sky showing my arrival are soon. They will be everywhere. The whole sky is going to light up."

"All shall see the darkness of three days: a plague of plagues. It shall cover the whole earth after a display of colorful dancing lights that covers sky to sky across your whole world."

"The cosmic event will cause the sky to glow and turn red, and everyone on the face of the earth will see this phenomenon. This is your warning to get others to stay indoors and get themselves prepared for the coming earthquake and darkness. My Father holds the timing for this."

The Bride of Christ

For it is the day of the Lord's vengeance, and the year of recompences for the controversy of Zion. Isaiah: 34:8 KJV.

How many times have you heard that the church is the bride of Christ? Well, whether you believe this to be true or not, the church is not the bride of Christ. We are the body of Christ, 1 Corinthians 12:27, Colossians 1:18 KJV. The bride of Christ is one woman, John 3-29, Mark 2:19, Revelation 21:9-11 KJV. Yahushua HaMashiach is both 100% man and 100% God. All things considered, being a man, He too is entitled to a bride, don't you think? And He calls her His wife, Revelation 19:7, 21:9 KJV. She has always been with Him. Song of Solomon 2:14, 6:9 KJV refers to her as **His** Dove (His Bride). But in John 1:32, Luke 3:22 KJV The Holy Spirit; **Spirit A** is also referred to as Dove. Well, His Dove: **Spirit B**, has also been incarnated into the earth; Her husband was born in a manger, Luke 2;7 KJV. She lives on the earth today and has now made herself ready to get married to Yahushua in the glorified flesh body, Revelation 19:7,8 KJV. The marriage supper of The Lamb takes place in Heaven, Revelation

19:8,9 KJV, but His marriage does not take place in Heaven. It takes place outside of Heaven in the Heavenly Jerusalem, Revelation 21:2,11 KJV. And when it arrives, the Lord will say to His beloved what is written in Song of Solomon 2:10-13 KJV. "My beloved spake, and said unto me, Rise up, my love, my fair one, and come away. For, lo, the winter is past, the rain is over and gone; The flowers appear on the earth; the time of the singing of birds is come, and the voice of the turtle is heard in our land; The fig tree putteth forth her green figs, and the vines with the tender grape give a good smell. Arise, my love, my fair one, and come away." It will be a spring wedding.

They are not getting married to benefit themselves because they have always been together. They are doing this to elevate marriage to its rightful position both in body and in spirit and to benefit us. She is the second Eve. She will fulfill that which Eve forfeited when she allowed herself to fall prey to temptation in the Garden of Eden, Genesis 3:1-7 KJV. She is New Jerusalem, a Nazarene and a member of the church of Philadelphia. Revelation 3:7,14:1 KJV. Her name is Wisdom, Proverbs 8:22-36 KJV. She is the principal: the nucleus of the 144000 daughters of Zion: The Key of David Isaiah 22:22 KJV. The Royal Daughter, Psalms 45:13-15 KJV, Mathew 25 KJV, along with Her husband Yahushua Ha Mashiach, Proverbs 4:7, Micah 4:6-12, Revelation 14:1 KJV. She and Yahushua were both on the cross together. She was inside of Him. She is the water that flowed from His side on Calvary, John 19:34 KJV. She is the Shulamite bride, Song of Solomon 6 KJV. She is Christ 'The Lord our Righteousness', Jeremiah 33:16 KJV, standing with Her husband. He is Christ 'The Lord our Righteousness', Jeremiah 23:6 KJV. She and Her husband are one. It's all part of the restoration of man since the fall in the Garden of Eden. These are the two olive trees, Zechariah 4:2-6,13,14 KJV, and the two candlesticks standing before the God of the earth, Revelation 11:3-12 KJV, (witnesses). The devil will try to destroy Her and the rest of the 144000 with Covid-19 vaccine, just like he did before in these two instances: Mathew 2:12-16 and Exodus 1:22 KJV. But Yahushua will rescue both her and them from the dragon, Revelation 12: 3-4, 6 KJV. Wisdom is His sister, Song of Solomon 5:2 KJV; and the antitype of Adam's Eve. Yet they can marry each other, just like us; the offsprings of Yahuveh if we are coming from different families. Yahushua and Wisdom were born of different mothers at different points in time, both incarnated: both begotten of the Father. Therefore, He is the begotten Son, and She is the begotten daughter: the Bride of Christ, both descendants of Eve just like you and I are. And in Yahushua's case, since the Godhead commanded all created living to reproduce after their own kind, then He too must follow His own command and marry Godkind, because He is Godkind. John 3:16 KJV says that Yahushua is the only begotten Son and Hebrew 1:6 KJV says that He is the first begotten. Therefore, the word FIRST implies that there is a second begotten, and the Word ONLY implies that there is not another begotten son, and that the second begotten is a daughter. She is our sister. Her name is Wisdom, Proverbs 8 KJV, but she is not manifested unto many. She must remain veiled to prevent us from idolizing Her. Yahushua will unveil Her for Himself when the time is right. Yes, this daughter of troops and judge was smitten upon the check (disrespected), Micah 5:1 KJV. But the response to this will be held back only up until the time when Assyria (the modern Christian World) including France, and the land of Nimrod (the United States of America-Mystery Babylon) is to be judged and wasted, Micah 5:4-6 KJV. Isaiah 34:8 KJV. The man-beast named Barack Hussein Obama, who promotes the number is 666 is not the antichrist. He is the false prophet, and along with the pope, will help Nimrod (Asshur); the antichrist beast who "shall ascends out of the bottomless pit and shall go into perdition ...." Revelation 17:8 KJV.

Yahushua and **Spirit A** is the Holy Spirit whose name is Revelation, Proverbs 6:20 KJV, and Jerusalem where the bride will dwell is the mother of us all, Galatians 4:26 KJV. Her husband; and our brother is our Redeemer and Her Redeemer, Romans 3:23 KJV. He paid His bride's price for both Her and us on the cross of Calvary. Proverbs 31:10 KJV. His name is Yahushua. This family is very protective of each other, Mathew 2:13 KJV, and we too must follow their example of family safeguard. Ephesians 1:17, and 1John 5:7-9 KJV speak about them. The Father bears record in Heaven, and **Spirit A**: The Holy Spirit bears witness on earth. Wisdom: **Spirit B**, the Holy Ghost Spirit is the water and Jesus the Word is the blood. His new name during the period of His intersession for us is THE BRANCH, Zechariah 6:12 KJV. And the Father, who is in Heaven, is named Yahawah. Notice here that there are four persons in the Godhead Family, not three as it's commonly believed to be. So now that you know the truth, please do not continue to leave out or ignore Wisdom the water Holy Ghost Daughter. It is an insult. That is like telling the Bride of Christ that you do not want to have anything to do with her. Be careful, She is the selected woman; Yahushua's help mate.

Most Bible students believe and refer to the Holy Spirit as one person only, but the above texts prove that there are two comforters; two persons who were never differentiated in the Old Testament, but for our benefit, they have been differentiated in the New Testament. We were made in the image and likeness of Yahuveh, and our families are patterned after the image and likeness of the Heavenly Family. So, to all you ladies out there who are saying that you are the Bride of Christ, having both earthly parents, STOP IT! You are mankind not Godkind. WAKE UP!

And now let us do all that we can with the help of the Holy Spirit to make it to the marriage supper of the Lamb, Revelation 19:6-9 KJV. And to all of us wise virgins invited to the wedding, let us consider ourselves plenty blessed, Mathew 25:1-13 KJV. It is almost time for the wedding. Almost time to go forth to meet Yahushua the bridegroom and Daughter Zion/Wisdom the bride. And when she leaves the earth to attend her nuptials, it will result in an earthquake and three days and three nights of darkness. This will be so because Yahushua; the light of the world, will be shut into the wedding chamber, along with His Bride who is judge in Israel, and with Her bridesmaids, John 8:12, Mathew 25:5-12 KJV. And He will not open the door to allow anyone in to disturb this event. "Let us be glad and rejoice and give Him glory, for the marriage of the Lamb has come, and His wife has made herself ready," Revelation 19:7 KJV. So be a wise virgin. Don't miss this Royal Wedding. Be there!

The Opening of the Sixth Seal: The Investigative Judgement of the Living

The sixth seal is opened at the onset of judgement upon Mystery Babylon (The United States of America), and upon the rest of the world. Revelation 6: 12-17 KJV reads, "And I beheld when he had opened the sixth seal, and, lo, there was a great earthquake; and the sun became black as sackcloth of hair, and the moon became as blood; And the stars of heaven fell unto the earth, even as a fig tree casteth her untimely figs, when she is shaken of a mighty wind. And heaven departed as a scroll when it is rolled together; and every mountain and island were moved out of their places. And the kings of the earth, and the great men, and the rich men, and the chief captains, and the mighty men, and every bondman, and every free man, hid themselves in the dens and in the rocks of the mountains; And said to the mountains and rocks, Fall on us, and hide us from the face of him that sitteth on the throne, and from the wrath of the Lamb: For the great day of his wrath is come; and who shall be able to stand?

There are quite a few events listed here at the

 37

opening of the sixth seal, none of which we have any control over. The only thing we can do is to get ready for these events and prepare.

Preparation Instructions for the Three Days and Nights of Darkness.

The most important preparation to make as you get ready for the three days and nights of darkness is to purify your own heart. Forgive all those who have hurt you. There should be no unforgiveness in your heart.

When you see the flashing bright lights of the aurora borealis in the sky, get into your houses immediately.

Use black plastic garbage bags and duct tape to cover your windows, because under no circumstances should you look out into the darkness. Neither should the darkness be allowed to penetrate your house if you can avoid it. Purchase these items now. Don't wait.

Let no stranger into your house. Do not open your doors to any familiar voice. No one can navigate themselves in such darkness. These are demons and devils. Revelation 9:14,15 KJV.

Use blankets to keep warm. If there is no sunlight, there will be no warmth. The picture below is just one example of how you can heat a space, using white scentless **bolsius** candles and a clay pot to create heat. Please purchase your candles and clay pots now. Don't wait.

Use white **bolsius** scentless candles as a source of light since electricity will go out.

Begin to stock up on food that needs no preparation, for example fruits, chips, nuts, and bread.

Stock up on drinking water now. Keep bottled water in your house to drink and to do simple toiletries.

Also keep buckets of water close to your toilet, to push down urine once in twenty-four hours before going to bed. Please collect your buckets now. Don't wait.

Plan how you will use the bathroom because the tanks cannot fill up without electricity. You can use biodegradable doggie bags for the brown stuff, then place them in a larger biodegradable garbage bag, or use kitty litter. Then bury everything in the ground when the sun returns. Please purchase these bags now. Don't wait.

There will be earthquakes, terrible confusion, and strange demonic voices in your surroundings during this time, but you cannot look outside in curiosity, Revelation 16:14-16 KJV, get ready.

The family is to quietly remain in one area of the house and not be walking up, down and around, all over the house at that time.

Wherever the darkness catches you at midday, get into a building and hunker down. Do not look or go outside under any circumstance.

Warn others that this is coming. It will give them a chance to get ready even though most likely they might not believe you, therefore they will be taken by surprise.

Keep your Bible close to you and stay in prayer. I carry a pocket Bible with me wherever I go. It is a good suggestion to have one in your possession too.

Many people do not know that these things are about to happen, but now that you know, please inform as many individuals as you can, so that there will be no blood on your hands.

Purchase unfermented grape juice and crackers or make your own unleavened bread, to take communion with your family when the darkness falls. Anoint your front and back doors and windows with blessed olive oil in the "**Sign of the Cross**" from now, and you can repeat this again if you choose to do so. It's a **PURIM** type judgement which comes with a blood moon, followed closely in a short space of time by three days and nights of gross darkness.

Cry to Yahuveh and His Son Yahushua for Mercy. He is our main protector. And stay safe. The **Highest**: The Most High be with us all at this time, is my prayer. I give Him all the glory!

"Come, my people, enter thou into thy chambers, and shut thy doors about thee: hide thyself as it were for a little moment, until the indignation be overpast. For, behold, the LORD cometh **out of his place** to punish the inhabitants of the earth for their iniquity: the earth also shall disclose her blood, and shall no more cover her slain," Isaiah 26:20, 21 KJV.

SECTION FOUR

The Infamous Earthquake and Tsunami: an Ezekiel 9 KJV type judgement Event.

Prophet Efraim Rodriguez

Based on the sequence of events written in Revelation 6;12-17 KJV, there will be a great earthquake hitting, just before this outer darkness from Tartarus, coupled with dark matter from CERN falls. The earthquake will be caused by an asteroid. The name of this rock is Churyumov–Gerasimenko abbreviated 67P. It is also called the Rosetta Comet nicknamed Chury. And the Most High has sent His messenger, PROPHET EFRAIM RODRIGUEZ, to give us the full details of this coming event.

This fiery Asteroid Falls at Night

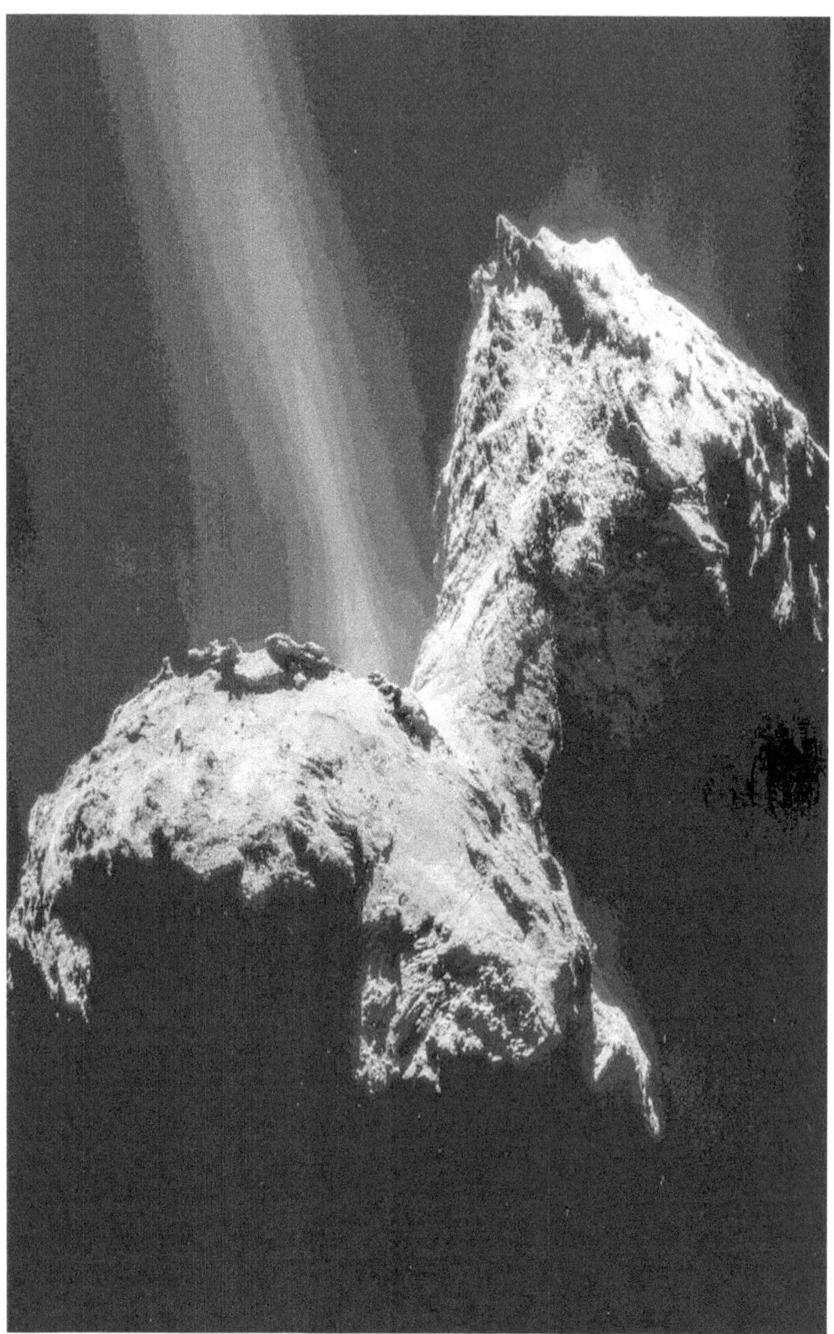

Asteroid Churyumov–Gerasimenko abbreviated 67P, also called the Rosetta Comet nicknamed Chury.

Comet 67 P is shaped like a duck.

The Sequence of Events

Just one suggestion though. If you have never seen the movie, "DEEP IMPACT" well, maybe this would be a good time to go watch it.

Revelation 18:21 KJV answers the question as to what this really is. It states, "And a mighty angel took up a stone like a great millstone, and cast *it* into the sea, saying, Thus with violence shall that great city Babylon be thrown down, and shall be found no more at all." Babylon here refers mainly to the United States of America (Mystery Babylon).

It is most important to know the sequence of events here, so that when things begin to happen, you will neither be confused nor afraid. Many will lose their lives. Therefore, instead of trying to run; *because you cannot run away from this*, use your final seconds and minutes to cry to Yah and His Son Yahushua in confession of your sins, repentance, and praise. "For whosoever will save his life shall lose it: and whosoever will lose his life for my sake shall find it. For what is a man profited, if he shall gain the whole world, and lose his own soul? or what shall a man give in exchange for his soul?" Mathew 16:25 KJV. Here is where you plead for Yahushua to show you mercy, and He will, because **HE IS MERCY!**

The sequence of events are as follows; -

1. A Catastrophic Asteroid Impact event.
2. A twelve-point earthquake. The number twelve here signifies that the entire Godhead will not be in Heaven at this time, but here on earth.
3. A nuclear shockwave explosion caused by the asteroid hit.
4. An extensive tsunami.
5. Three days and nights of darkness.

It's an Extinction Level Event!

The Trajectory of Asteroid 67P

Based on information given by Prophet Rodriguez, Nasa scientists have gone to Puerto Rico and taken hold of the radar there, the biggest observatory of its kind. They have taken it away from the local scientists because they started seeing what was foretold by the prophet. As they monitored the situation, asteroids began to be seen on root to earth, such as what happened in

Arecibo Observatory in Puerto Rico

Russia. About fifteen hundred people were hurt in that country, because people were not informed of this incoming danger and where the asteroid would hit.

The prophet speaks: – "The rock will be entering Puerto Rican skies early in the morning at 2.00 AM. This will be the beginning of the judgement of God upon the earth. It will be entering the skies above Arecibo and will exit through Mayaguez; and will finally make impact between Mayaguez and the island of Mona to the west of Puerto Rico. There is no way of escaping from this wrath of God here in Puerto Rico or in the United States. When this asteroid makes impact it will generate a nuclear explosion. The Lord has revealed to many people, that there will be experts in body suits dealing with this after the event, similar to what happened in Japan with the thermo- nuclear facility. He has also revealed to people in Puerto Rico that after the event, unusual activity will be seen. When the scientist saw this message, they called me to enquire for further information about the nuclear explosion and other details. I simply told them, that will be the trajectory of the asteroid.

The Most High will not make any changes, because He is the one who controls space and everything else. I told them also to keep vigilant because according to a scientist, a nuclear explosion will be originated at a dept of four hundred feet below sea level, on the trench under water in that area. They checked their maps and told me that the underwater dept of the area of impact is 400 feet. I said, thank you Lord for that. Thank you, thank you Lord. They were stunned because they saw that I was joyful. I told them that I was, because if this asteroid was to hit in the area north or south of Puerto Rico, where the sea floor is much deeper, none of us would live to tell it. This is a partial judgement, not a total one. The islands would not sink. To answer the question of one of the scientists. I told them that there would be a twelve-point earthquake. A twelve-point earthquake would be something never before seen no matter what scale you use. It would be supernatural.

The asteroid's dimensions are big. Right now, there is an asteroid on route to earth, which is making all the scientists really really nervous. They are currently preparing astronauts and weapon systems just like in the movies. That is why they halted the space program in order to concentrate on these preparations. This happened after they received a message not so long ago. I told the scientist, you will not understand what twelve points mean, but the church of Christ listening to this presentation will understand. I hope the presence of the Holy Spirit is with you as I speak to you, so that you get confirmation from the Lord, and you are able to tell your family. Give them the message in writing, not verbally. There are too many details concerning this message, and they have to be read in writing. The Lord has decreed this judgement, and the message has all the details pertaining to His judgement. The scientists gave me some information that put me in a state of alarm. They told me about the shockwave generated by such an impact. You will see what they are talking about on the footage of what happened in Russia. You will see how a much minor shockwave affected a whole area in Russia. The scientist told me this asteroid shockwave will travel at three hundred miles per hour, which is very very serious brothers and sisters. Brothers and sisters, a shock wave travelling at three hundred miles an hour is like two hurricanes mixed together. This has never before been seen on earth. According to the Lord, when this earthquake starts, it will shake the United States too. The Lord says that He will wake the United States at the time of impact at that time of the morning simultaneously with Puerto Rico. Why? The United States has a record to settle with Him. They have currently changed the laws that dictated morality for immoral laws. The one insisting that all laws be changed favoring abnormal behavior, is the president of the nation himself. He knows that this angers God. He pushes judges who have to do with passing laws to approve new laws quickly and urgently. He knows The Most High is angry. Everything immoral is being approved in that nation supported by law. Currently, this president in conjunction with the army's chief security, has forbidden soldiers to speak about HaMashiach anywhere in the army. They are not allowed to pray, or to speak about Yahushua under penalty of being demoted or thrown into jail if they fail to obey this mandate. He has done many things already shown in the media. He is an immoral president. He knows that he has an agenda from hell and is helping out the enemy in this hellish endeavor. I will only say that the time remaining for him is short. The Lord of Heaven will do justice, not man. Believe me, wherever they hide, they will not escape the wrath of God either. The church contributes to this by helping them, by accepting human laws instead of the laws of the Word, and thus pollute the temples and churches, marrying men with men and women with women. The church is part of this already. Very, very few churches step up and say "no" the Bible does not say so. What has been written has to be fulfilled and nobody will stop it. These are the events for this judgement. I want you to know that the government of the United States already has estimates. We will have a nuclear explosion never before seen in that area. We will get a twelve-point earthquake after impact. Scientists confirm this for our area. Puerto Rico will be the epicenter of this judgement, not anywhere else. I challenge anyone who has the true presence of the Lord to prove me wrong. And if you think I have a spirit of error or deception, I challenge you, if you have true presence of the Holy Spirit within you, to come and rebuke me, because I guarantee you that the Most High sent me to deliver this message. I get no financial gain or seek no personal gain with this. I have to obey the Lord's command. He broke down my health, and I prefer that He does anything to me and not men. I prefer His hand be upon me than a man's hand. No matter what happens, I will declare the whole judgement. I will let the church know what those twelve points mean. The following is the reason why, as I told the scientists, the islands won't sink because of the earthquake or impact.

This is a judgement prior to the events in Revelation, to shape up the church around the world, to be able to take the gospel of Mashiach to all the countries, that nowadays do not allow the gospel to enter their land. They will be in awe of the situation because the Lord made this message to travel the whole world first. That is what He told me on that morning, "My servant, send this message to the whole world with every detail beforehand, so that they would know that it was I who executed this judgement, because nowadays others want to take the credits." No, The Highest One spoke first. The scientists will be saying what He already dictated, confirming that something is indeed approaching the earth. That is the greatness of the message. All glory will go to The Holy One of Israel. That is why we come to this nation in tears, leaving behind our families back home. The Lord opened the doors for us to come here, since this country did not know about this event. It is very possible that your leaders may know, but they cannot say anything at this point, and we agree with that. But the church has a supreme leader, and we do this even though we respect the laws and the land, but the Lord above wants to inform His church here and everywhere we go of His plans, so that we prepare before that dark night comes upon us.

Deep Impact

The asteroid will produce a thousand-foot wave at the point of impact. According to the scientists we spoke to, this wave will be travelling at approximately four hundred miles per hour. At four hundred miles per hour, many areas of Puerto Rico will be covered by the sea as you will

67 P will Produce an Earthquake and a Thousand-Foot Wave upon Impact, Travelling at Approximately Four Hundred Miles Per Hour.

When this Asteroid Makes Impact, it will Generate a Nuclear Explosion.

see in the next map. (*Another map is provided further on in this account to show the results of this asteroid impact.*) In addition, the land of Puerto Rico will be swaying like a drunkard. The whole continent will be trembling like never before. The wave that you will see will travel towards the United States. The Dominican Republic will be the second country to be hit. Members of the government informed me that they have an estimate of human casualties due to this event. They opened up to me because I gave them information that no one else has. They clearly told me that they have an estimate of two point five million losses of life just for Puerto Rico. The majority of the church of HaMashiach in Puerto Rico has turned against this message. Supposedly they have the presence of His Spirit among them. The Lord left us the presence of the Holy Spirit to help us, to guide us, to take care of us one hundred percent, and to deliver us, prepared and worthy for the Lord at His return. It seems the church threw this presence out. They do not ask Holy Spirit if this is from the Lord or not. In Puerto Rico, there are about six thousand churches. Most of them mocked the Lord, that is why He told me, "My servant, the church has added to the amount of debts," which means the situation will be even worse.

There was hope that the church would receive this message and heed its warning, as the sinful city of Nineveh did when the prophet Jonah warned them. We brought the message and most places, they mocked it. The government is preparing for this, yet the church says that the Most High cannot do such a thing. It is contradictory. But I tell you that what the non-believers are preparing for is what will come to pass. Even they, although not serving the Father, believe in this more than the church, because what they see fills them with fear and terror. The church of Puerto Rico believes this was a fairy tale, just as they labelled it in a very well-known ministry in Puerto Rico. They told me this was a literary tale. If they only knew that this literary tale is about to come to pass. There is not much time left. The government agent, whose identity I cannot reveal, showed us a log with the amounts of estimated deaths per each municipality, really high numbers. As I told you before, the government's total estimate is

2.5 million deaths in Puerto Rico. The plastic coffins for the bodies have arrived both in the United States and in Puerto Rico. FEMA is currently preparing Puerto Rico for a possible earthquake and tsunami. They are storing water, food, and giving presentations about evacuation. The difference is that they cannot tell people about the third event, because that event comes from the Lord.

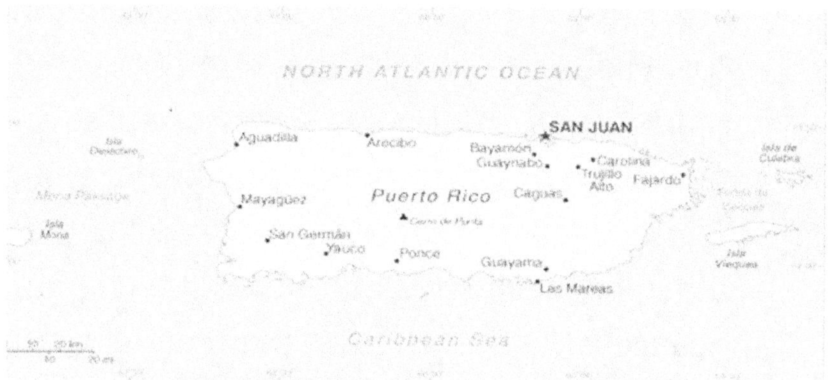

Map of Puerto Rico

The rock will be in the hands of the Most High that night. He will toss it upon the earth, and it will fall on the sea. That difference is what has scientists in fear.

Right now, there are thousands and thousands of asteroids around and close to the earth, but prior to the rapture, only one event will befall the earth. That night, Yahushua Ha Mashiach must do something different for Him to prepare His church. The world will be in awe and terror at what He will do. Right now, they are perplexed because the situation is clear, specific, and there is no change in the route that they are seeing towards the earth. *Scientists* have indicated that this impact will stop the rotation of the earth for three days. These are real, not fictional scientists. The fact that the earth's rotation will stop for three days is a terrible thing for us. That's why I indicated that the twelve points means that The Father, The Son, and the Holy Spirit will be on earth that night, touching the ground in Puerto Rico at the time of this execution.

Half Hour Silence in Heaven

"And when he had opened the seventh seal, there was silence in heaven about the space of half an hour. And I saw the seven angels which stood before God; and to them were given seven trumpets. And another angel came and stood at the altar, having a golden censer; and there was given unto him much incense, that he should offer it with the prayers of all saints upon the golden altar which was before the throne. And the smoke of the incense, which came with the prayers of the saints, ascended up before God out of the angel's hand. And the angel took the censer, and filled it with fire of the altar, and cast it into the earth: and there were voices, and thunderings, and lightnings, and an earthquake," Revelation 8:1-5 KJV.

1. The silence divides the two pre-millennial Judicial sessions, the one for the dead and the other for the living, and the fire from the heavenly altar, the voices, lightnings, and thunderings, descend to earth. These facts, along with a number of scriptures on the subject, besides the remainder of The Revelation, the chapters after the breaking of the seventh seal, prove that the Judgment of the living, the cleansing of the earthly temple, is something which takes place on earth, not in heaven only!

"Behold," declares the Lord, "I will send My messenger, and he shall prepare the way before Me: and the Lord, Whom ye seek, shall suddenly come to His temple,..... But who may abide the day of His coming? and who shall stand when He

V. T Houteff, The Shepherds Rod, Tract 15, 64.[1]

appeareth? for He is like a refiner's fire, and like fullers' soap." Mal. 3:1 KJV.

2. Yes, the work of the second Judicial session includes the earthly sanctuary, the church. At that time the Lord's "fire" is in Zion and His furnace in Jerusalem Isa. 31:9 KJV.

The pre-millennial Investigative Judgement of Daniel 7:9,10 KJV is divided into two sections; first to investigate the dead and then to investigate the living. It is quite different from the post-millennial Great White Throne judgement of the wicked in Revelation 20:11-15 KJV. And when the investigative judgement of the dead in the Heavenly Sanctuary, found in Daniel 8:13,14 KJV is completed, then the investigative judgement of the living commences first on earth, to cleanse the church here on earth. This is what results in a half hour (one week) silence in Heaven. At that time, the Godhead and Heavenly angels are on earth to complete the task. Once this phase of investigation is accomplished, it continues and is finished in the Heavenly sanctuary, after the half hour silence noted above.

V. T Houteff, The Shepherds Rod. [2]

The prophet speaks: - "The presence of The Highest of Heaven; The Most High of the universe will be upon the earth. He will not be on His throne at the time of this execution. He will be touching the ground in Puerto Rico.

His army is ready to descend. There are already hordes of Heaven on earth marking the flock that will be set apart for this judgement. The believers to whom I am speaking should understand me. This is serious. Thus says the Lord. These are not fairy tales; I am speaking seriously. I could be home right now with my children and grandchildren, but the Lord showed me this, and my duty is to present it and take it to the world. I fled from this message until three years ago, when I started delivering it. Not for a hundred and twenty years like Noah. It seems people have forgotten about that. We have delivered this message for three years, and many have not taken it seriously. They have mocked it and forgotten. After three years they are tired of it. Remember that when Noah finished the ark, the Lord told him, "In seven days this will be over. Fill the ark with food and enter into it with the animals and your family." The Lord gave Noah a date. In seven days. Here, the minutes are also running out. For forty-one years, the Holy Spirit has been revealing to me that a great war was coming. But I knew the church would go astray. In the past, every time Israel went astray, the Lord would discipline them. He would send them death and pestilence. This today is the final church, the church of the end times; the generation that would see the Lord Christ. That is why the Lord warns them with full details.

When the scientist told me about the three days during which the rotation of the earth would stop, they alarmed me even more. I'll tell you why, because of the corpses left behind in Puerto Rico and in this area of the Caribbean, whether on earth or in the water. The United States will be hit after 5:00 A.M. The wave will hit the area of Miami first. The United States is not playing around. There are serious evacuation procedures and preparations for the whole east coast. The Most High will sweep the area clean. The places where most festivals and parades occur, playing with and celebrating immorality. These are located mainly on the coastlines. God will sweep them. The United States is preparing boxes for

Module One: This Tsunami will hit Puerto Rico, Santo Domingo, the US beginning from Miami and all the areas of the Caribbean.

millions of corpses. They have burners to dispose of the bodies after the event. They also have mobile homes for the people left homeless. They are storing enormous amounts of food, and emergency supplies in the middle of the nation, for a minimum of fifteen months of need after the event. The rest of the world is also preparing. All the islands around Puerto Rico will also be hit.

Witchcraft runs a mock on these islands. There is human sacrifices going on all of our islands. They are sacrificing human lives to the enemy. Men and women who at one point knew the Lord and then went astray, warlocks, witches, and satanic priest. In Puerto Rico, there is a whole area in the western part of the island, where these kinds of sacrifices are carried on continually, everywhere in the mountains, and nobody can do anything about it, because they are people with high ranks and positions in the government: politicians. It is important for you to understand that the whole island of Puerto Rico has become polluted as I'm sure is also the case with this island. The warlocks and witches are the owners in most cases. The churches are surrounded by them, and by satanic priest who curse the church every day.

They come into our churches. We went to a church in San Juan where a witch tried to come in while I was saying the corresponding prayer that we always pray. She came in and could not resist the presence of The Holy One of Israel and had to exit. She would try again and would have to leave. She could not stay. There was presence of The Highest there. That is how they infiltrate our temples. Since many churches no longer have the presence of the Lord, these people infiltrate the churches, carrying Bibles under their arms, and they curse us. Even in my church in Camote, one of them has constantly come in, and no one confronts him, because they have tossed the presence of the Holy Spirit aside. This is why the United States prepares the nation for this asteroid hit. They know the epicenter is Puerto Rico, not somewhere else. Father has already singled out this island and pointed His figure at it.

From Puerto Rico the true gospel spread elsewhere. also, to this island Santo Domingo, and many other countries. He prospered us with abundance and gave us everything in a few years. The prosperity of Puerto Rico's success was such that when the US was lacking food, Puerto Rico still had enough, because the Most High of the universe controlled the situation. There was a hedge of protection from angels all around Puerto Rico protecting the island. But the Lord slowly began removing those angels because the church started slowly going astray.

And now they still ask, "Why is the Lord going to do this to us?" It has been established, and nobody can change it. Ask Him, and ask yourself where you have fallen from, each of you. Why is there so much evil in Puerto Rico and all over. Why is there no security on our land. All kinds of evil, **all kinds of evil** homosexual parades. Right now, the government of Puerto Rico approved a law to be signed by the governor of Puerto Rico, in favor of what according to them is an endangered species: the homosexuals. They want special laws as if they were becoming extinct. The Bible says the opposite. It says that it would be as in the times of Noah, there will be everything. On the contrary they are growing in numbers. I only tell you, enjoy those laws while you have them because there is very little time remaining for those laws. The church is still on earth, and nobody will touch it because it belongs to the

Lord. You can do whatever you want, but the church is untouchable.

The political leaders in Puerto Rico smile to themselves with these people who have blasphemed the Word and the commandment of Yahushua. Go and multiply were His Words to Adam and Eve. They want to multiply with members of the same sex. They are gravely mistaken. In a short while they would die, and the earth would be left empty if they had their way. But the earth will not be left empty, because there are still men and women who believe in the words and mandates of the Holy One of Israel. Male and female, that's how they entered the Ark, that is why there are animals nowadays. That was the order given to Noah by Yah. Multiply, grow, that is the Lord's command, and that word would not be altered by anyone! So, enjoy the laws you have currently, because soon you will not have them. The church will depart at a given moment, but Yahushua will give her peace, in order to be able to rescue the millions of souls that need to be saved within this trial. It is important that you know this.

This map of Puerto Rico shows how the sea will

come inland that night. I challenge anyone who has the Holy Spirit present in them to testify otherwise. We here are governed by that Spirit. We do what the Holy Spirit tells us. When there's danger He warns us, "Do not go through there." Sometimes He tells us "Do not leave the room or do not leave the house." He is the one who knows where danger is, and He defends us from the traps and evil of the enemy.

FEMA already has the map of Puerto Rico. From the United Nations they estimate millions of deaths. There is an estimate of forty million deaths in the area including Puerto Rico, Santo Domingo, the US and all the areas of the Caribbean. The preparations being made are on a scale only seen before in movies. Those movies are a vivid example of what would come to pass in our time, not another time. To those who are within the church and say this is not so because they lack the presence of the Holy Spirit, I tell them that I guarantee you, you will see this unless…and may the Holy Spirit bring you out of your error, so that you can prepare. You do not know this, but the preparations being done by the US right now are gigantic. The army's aircrafts

Module Two: Puerto Rico is the Epicenter of this Tsunami.

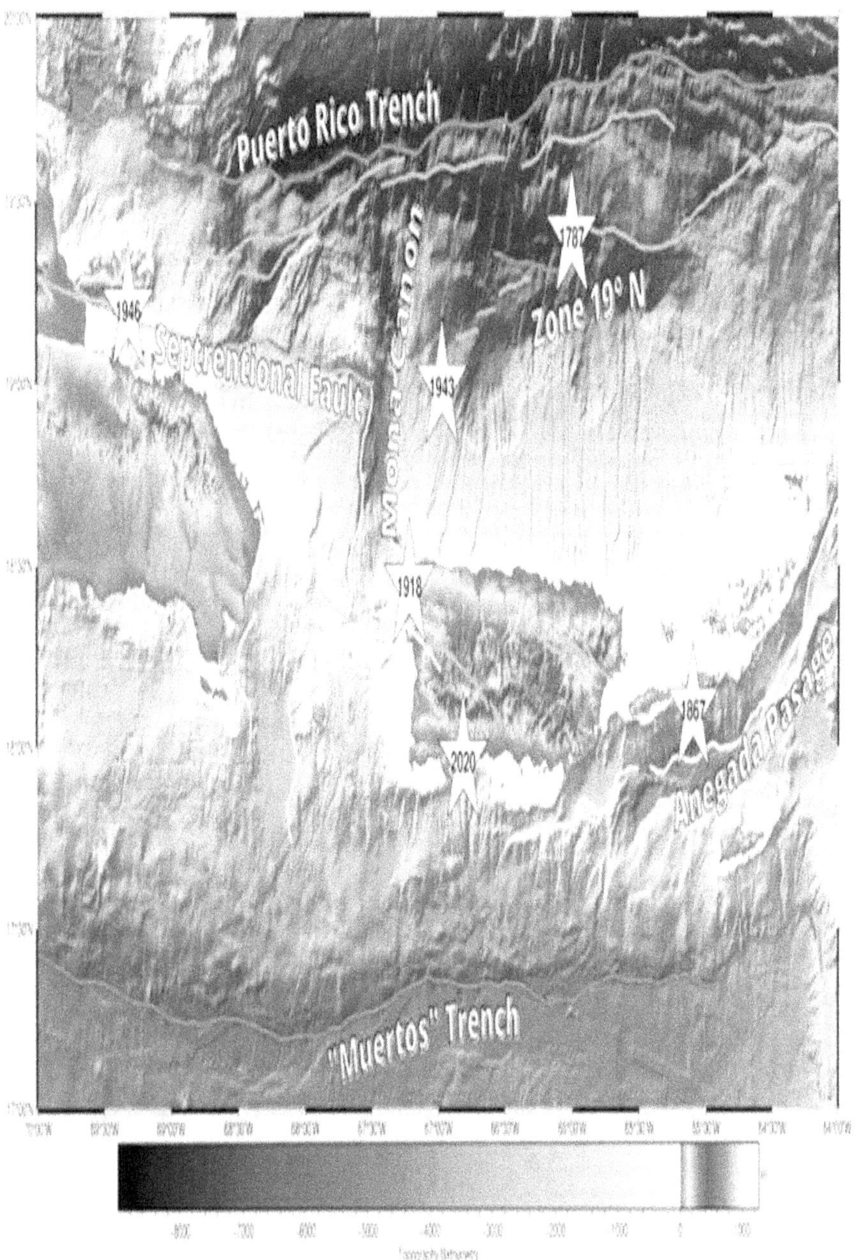

To the North there is the Subduction Zone Associated with the Puerto Rico Trench, to the West there is the Extensional Zone that forms the Mona Canyon.

are being moved to a place in the Pacific. Yahushua will allow them to know the time. He keeps allowing the representatives of science to know, and He has not violated this. The difference is that the Father Himself would let His people know. He would let the church who is ready and alert on that night know; the people who serve the Lord with a true heart. He would preform miracles for those who cannot move from where they are. You have to claim His protection as explained in the written message.

When Yahushua speaks in this manner, it is not as some say, "to instill fear." On the contrary, it is to let us know so that we can prepare before the event happens. You need to understand that the love of The Most High is so great that He warns us beforehand. Japan was not warned as I said before. Indonesia was not warned either. Many children died. Many will also die in our land: children, the elderly, people, animals. Brothers and sisters, we think that what happened in Japan, in Indonesia and other places could never happen here because we are Yah's pretty spoiled children. We are wrong. They are coming to settle accounts because of the abundance we were given. As you can see on the map, the sea will reach areas in the mountains where things happen that do not please the Lord. There is an overabundance of evil in those places that are shaded, especially on the plains like Sodom and Gomorrah, where people do things that they consciously know are against the Word. The Word of the Lord has been taken to every corner of Puerto Rico. It is the country that knows Yahushua Ha Mashiach the most in all areas, and it is full of backsliders and apostates of the faith. Now they say that Yahushua is not coming, and many other things. They tell their members, "Come, there is prosperity here, abundance keeps overflowing." Few days remain for them, very little time left.

Three days of darkness are coming according to the scientists. Three days of darkness for Puerto Rico, the United States, and the Caribbean. Total darkness for the whole continent for three days. This is not good news. This means that for three days, bodies would not be able to be disposed of by using the body bags or black boxes. This means bodies would start decomposing in Puerto Rico, Santo Domingo, the US and everywhere else affected by this. If the estimates of deaths for Puerto Rico is over two million, ask yourself, what will the number be here? Ask this question before our Lord. Many people who have spoken to me have been given revelations by the Most High of an infinite amount of corpses. Analyze spiritually if the Holy Spirit has declared and spoken to you personally, so you can start preparing urgently. Start asking for forgiveness from your family members. Start making peace with as many as you can. Start rescuing souls by giving them the message in written form, whether you or they believe or not, all should read it. The Lord knows their heart.

There are already pits dug that have been dug up for the corpses in Puerto Rico; something never before seen just like what we saw down in Haiti for corpses of men, women and children to be thrown in together like animals. I saw that with my own eyes. I said "Lord, so many people: people with souls. Where are the souls of all those people now, did they go with you?" Those five hundred thousand souls approximately who died within a minute. They were taken by surprise; we, however, will not be taken by surprise. We have the glorious Mashiach whom we accept. We always emphasize that. Only He can help us, only Him. I accept Him as my only and exclusive Savior, always confess this. Outside of Him, no one will help you, only Him. We must always ask the Father in Yahushua's name so that He grants us our request.

Yahushua is the one interceding for us right now. He did not intercede for the Japanese, and they were taken by surprise. They were possibly Christians over there, and we trust He did them justice. But over there is an abundance of idolatry. They pray and ask of Buddha who cannot respond. He is mute. Our Lord, however, does respond. That is why He tells us beforehand of His plans. He lets us know ahead of time what He intends to do on this earth. In Puerto Rico, some ten hospitals were secretly prepared in the mountains. Medical doctors were hired for the aftermath of the event, if they are able to come out of the buildings, (if The Most High does not bury them during the event,) so they can help the wounded with first aid care. This is a good thing; however, they need to seek the Lord's counsel first. They are only looking at the select group without consulting the Lord. A group of about forty thousand families were told in advance so they could start making arrangements to move to the mountains, renting or buying land or homes to preserve the race, according to them. But they are solely mistaken. There are a group of righteous servants of the Lord in many places, and the Lord we serve will let them know in advance, just like He did with Lot, so they can move to places of safety in the mountains. The angels told Lot to hurry because nothing could be done until Lot and His family left the city. The Lord of Heaven does wonders for the sake of the people who honor Him.

Recently, on one of our visits to a church in this country, a young woman approached me to ask me for guidance. She said she had a problem and did not want to be lost without the Lord. She said she was living with someone, and they were not married. She is in fornication, a common thing within the church. When they listen to a message as this one, many feel fear in their hearts. That fear is necessary in order for them to get right with the Lord. I asked her, "Do you love your boyfriend?" She said yes. "Does he love you?"

she said yes. "Then get married," I said. What is approaching is bound to affect a change into us living life the way Yahushua wants us to live it. A life of holiness to the best we can, although we have faults. The Lord knows our faults. This young woman wants to set things right with the Lord before this happens. I told her, "Go and get married by the state first, then make arrangements to get married by the church. In that way, you will be obeying the laws of earth and the laws of heaven. The Lord will re-establish you, do this quickly."

The same thing goes on in Puerto Rico, fornication between youngsters and adults is abundant. And then they go up into the Holy Place, into the altars in front of the church congregation. There is an abundance of this in our land. That is why the Lord is angry and that's why He will send this terrible judgement. This message is already present all over the world in places where there is true presence of The Most High through the Holy Spirit. All sorts of terrible things are going on within our churches. People carrying Bibles, speaking in tongues, dancing, yet they are not from the Lord. They deceive many because people do not ask the Lord to show them the truth. Many speak tongues from the altars, and people immediately claim that person is godly. No, you have to analyze carefully, asking the Holy Spirit. This is happening in Puerto Rico.

Recently, we received a call from a sister from one of the churches we had not too long ago visited. She said that on the day we went to her church, she had already made the decision to leave the church, until she heard this message and felt hope again. She then decided to call us and tell us about the following situation. An evangelist started prophesying to her telling her that she had a ministry and that the Lord would bless greatly. But he said the Lord had told him to go to her house and anoint her with oil. He told this young woman that she had to be alone in the house because he had to anoint her from head to toe with oils over her whole body. You see this? People using the Word, the speaking of tongues which are not of Yah to perform these aberrations. A pastor in Puerto Rico abusing his own four sons for years, even as grownups. He is in jail right now and still preaching. Several Pentecostal homosexual pastors are married with children. What do we expect? That is how things are in Puerto Rico and in this country too. Then they say that a judgement such as this cannot come. If the Lord didn't do this, the flocks would be lost. We lose heart because we see nobody doing anything. Pastors looking the other way when sin is right in front of their eyes, just because they do not want to lose the offerings and tithes of their church members. The Most High will provide, but you cannot allow sin to go on in the churches. You will never hunger. The Word establishes this truth. If the Word is taken as the Lord commands, He would provide, regardless of tithes and offerings. However, they do not want to make an effort. They are afraid of suffering loss and lack. That is why sin runs a mock in our temples, in our churches.

This message is for the church. This judgement comes because of the church, not the non-believers. The church has to step out and go look for the neighbors; the ones who have gone astray. You have to do the work. We are taking this message to Puerto Rico, Santo Domingo, and anywhere else where the Lord sends us, to tell people about the few minutes we have before His plans come to pass. These minutes are in His time, not ours. The body pits in Puerto Rico clearly indicate that the US is preparing. However, it would be very difficult under the circumstances to bury corpses in bags. That is why we have to be completely bound to the Holy Spirit before, during and after this trial. Very difficult days are coming, during and after. As the scientists told me, "If the earth's rotation stops, we would be entering an epidemic, because bodies would lie undisposed of for three days." We need to be bound to Yahushua, so that the Holy Spirit keeps a hedge of protection around us against the pestilence and all the events that will occur afterwards.

The Mountains in Las Marias and Maricao Puerto Rico (PR)

Warlocks and witches preform sacrifices in these mountains; the government knows about it. In these mountains, belonging to the municipality of Las Marias and Maricao in Puerto Rico and in other areas, is where there is an abundance of such rituals. Nobody enters these lands. It is difficult mountain terrain with no direct access to

Warlocks and Witches Preform Sacrifices in the Mountains of Las Marias and Maricao PR.

the areas where these rituals are performed, on altars dedicated to human sacrifice. There are women in Puerto Rico, some college university students, who sell their womb for five thousand dollars because of their financial needs. These satanist take advantage of that. They are all politicians of all parties; doctors, judges, satanic priest, and members of all sections and degrees of society. They are all part of this customary practice. That is why the Lord will destroy and wash those mountains with the sea. When the nuclear explosion occurs at the point of impact between Mayaguez and the island of Mona, the resulting 1000 ft. wave would be covering this whole area. These satanic people will all be congregated together in these areas that night. Yahushua will cleanse this whole area that you see. They are full of trees. You would soon see it completely cleared up. The spilt blood will all go to the sea. Hopefully, those of you who are spared by the Lord will see it through satellites, etcetera.

The whole territory of Puerto Rico belongs to The Lord. He comes to perform a counter offensive to restore the land of Puerto Rico. He told me, "My servant, I will later make multitudes return to Puerto Rico to repopulate it." The estimate of deaths given by the government will be the actual one. "More than two and a half million people will die in Puerto Rico," The Lord told me, and I hope you get this. He told me clearly that the majority of the church in Puerto Rico will die that night of judgement. He will execute the church. I challenge anyone in Puerto Rico or elsewhere, if they have true presence of the Holy Spirit, to come and testify that this is not so, because I hope the Holy Spirit confirms to you what I am saying here. If any of you in this nation know any Christians in Puerto Rico, you need to ask if they will be under this execution. If they are not doing the Lord's work as is stated by Him, then they'll get theirs, here and there. However, the majority of the church in Puerto Rico will be new.

The Lord told me, "My servant, I will bring forth a new flock in Puerto Rico." The Lord has discarded the majority of the church in Puerto Rico. Six thousand churches in such a small territory. Most of them have tossed aside this message from Him saying that He will not, and will not do this, and that. They will not spread the message or divulge it, because they do not want to instill fear in the people. They are disobeying the order that Yahushua gave to Jonah, to warn the city of Nineveh of an upcoming judgement. The members of Nineveh spread the word and warned each other. The church, however, having the Holy Spirit does not warn each other. Unbelievable! Having the presence of the Lord yet they are afraid. What do you think will happen. They disobeyed the mandate of Ezekiel 33 KJV, where it says the watchman sees danger, and is required to sound the alarm. In Ezekiel chapter 34, those same shepherds faced execution. In the same manner, The Godhead comes to demand from the pastors, "What did you do with my church, where are the ones that have gone astray, and why did you not go after them looking for them. Where are the ones that were wounded, why did you not send healing words; guidance?" That's the state of the church in Puerto Rico, full of people who have gone astray with no one to go after them. That is why They come in Person. I have spoken serious words. If I was speaking a false word saying thus said the Lord, that would mean death for me spiritually. I am still alive. My life would be in danger of Hell Fire if I spoke words that Yahushua did not say, while saying "Thus says the Lord." I have no desire to go down there nor plan to do so. That is why I am obeying the Lord to deliver this message to this nation and to Puerto Rico, as we have been doing for three years.

The church who claims they are the church of The Most High in Puerto Rico will never be seen again. The Lord will bring in a new church from a small remnant that will remain alive from the current church. The authorities say that more than 2 1/2 million people will die out of the approximate 3.8 million inhabitants in Puerto Rico, even though they will deny it and will not publish those figures as we are doing right now. As the moment approaches, they have started speaking out alerting the people little by little. However, the Lord has sent a spirit of error even to the believers so that they keep thinking He would not do this. He will execute them for the reasons mentioned above. They abandoned the true part, fell into apostasy, and left the faith. The Lord keeps sending them a lying spirit so that they think His presence is still in the churches, but He is nowhere near those places. They would be deceived as were Ahab's prophets as exposed by Micaiah.

The king's prophets said one thing, but Michiah said something else. I would speak as Micaiah. A great woe approaches the earth, and it will be the triple event that Yahushua will bring to pass that night. All the presidents of the different nations besides the US know about this, but we will continue our work until the event happens. We will not abandon anything. We will continue our work; our plans but staying alert to the moment when the Lord tells us to leave and to move. We cannot avoid His wrath or run from it. If it were up to me, I would like to move to the US, we could easily do it, but I won't, because maybe if I do, I will end up dying over there. I'll stay here, waiting for the Holy Spirit's instructions, because I do know where I'll be that night with my family, that is why I have no problem with staying. There's a guarantee of protection for me and for any others who come on board. The Lord is so good that He declares His plans and intentions, prior to the chastisement so that we can rectify spiritually. Understand this! We need to fill ourselves with spiritual oil which is the presence of the Lord. After this priority, we can anoint our homes, possessions, etcetera. The primary guarantee is ourselves before the Lord. Everything else will be added by Him.

The United States will be going through the same crisis as us. For that reason, the Holy Spirit told me, "My servant, I have set aside a nation that will bring nourishment to you first." Believe me, there will be a massacre, death, never before seen. There will be a triple judgement event. It has to be this way, otherwise nobody will make a change in their lives. Only The Most High Himself could straighten out the church, by acting in favor of the postulates that Ha Mashiach died for on the Cross of Calvary. Otherwise, unless He does this, no one would turn to Yahushua. The Father spoke to me about a nation that would come to our aide. In the written message, I included a paragraph about the man who was the leader of this nation. The Lord told me that I, as well as many, will be greatly surprised when He reveals the name of the nation. He told me that the nation whom the Lord chose to bring food to us first, would be Venezuela.

Before dying, Hugo Chavez, the then president of Venezuela declared publicly on TV, certain statements after the Lord had already given me this message of warning. Many believers and people from the government of Puerto Rico were witnesses to President Chavez's statement and confirmed this. Chavez said, "If you are truly God, heal me. You know that I am saving food for many people, and I want to be the one to deliver it in person." He cried to Yahushua based on his situation, and after having cursed the chosen nation in a previous statement. He cursed Israel publicly. He was now crying to Yahushua because he was sick. We always look to Him when we are in trouble, when we are sick hypocritically, no sincerity. Sincerity is what the Lord wants. You might have gone astray, but if you come to the Lord with sincerity, He would bring you back. He would show you mercy, He will help you.

Chavez was not sincere. He waited too late and did not say the words he needed to say. He had to declare certain things publicly. He needed to take back things he had said and apologize. The wise man knows to rectify. This man has nothing to do with this prophecy. His words simply confirmed what Yahushua showed me about Venezuela; the nation chosen and ordained by the Lord Himself to help us first after the impact. Thus declared Yah. Hugo Chavez himself had nothing to do with the prophecy unless the Lord had healed him, which did not happen, so the prophecy stands. Some say that the prophecy is untrue because Chavez died. False! He has nothing to do with the message. Read the message carefully so you can understand what it stated. Do not twist Yahushua's words, like they are doing by negotiating holiness as a requisite to see the Lord. The churches and the media have sold out the Word. Messages that speak about Mashiach are not allowed anymore, even less about the rapture and even less about a coming judgement. They only broadcast on TV and radio programs and messages that bring them gain, messages about prosperity and not any other kind of messages that does not bring them profit.

Dollar by dollar, the church saved enough throughout the years to purchase these radio and

TV stations to broadcast the Word. Over fourteen stations in Puerto Rico. All of them have sold out the message. I have news for you. The Highest of Heaven will destroy them with His feet when He walks over the land of Puerto Rico that night. All ministries will fail; all, no exceptions. They would all be destroyed, even the ones we understood were the most holy. They sold out. As we can all see, their broadcasts have become completely polluted. Yahushua will show more mercy to the unbelievers that night than to the Christians, because sometimes they believe more than the actual believer's, who have the presence of the Holy Spirit at their disposal, yet they mock The Most High. They mock the Lord's sacrifice.

Missiles have been set up in different parts of Puerto Rico, to attempt to destroy the asteroid as it approaches. We know that there are nuclear submarines. We don't know where they are ready for action. All is ready in Puerto Rico by orders of the president to help us prior to the impact, since he will not be able to come to our aide after the impact for a while, just like Yahushua said. He sent millions of boxes of dry food through the army for us to have nourishment after the cataclysm. They had initially stored body bags, food and supplies in the coastal areas. I told the governor to move them to the mountains, because if he kept them near the sea, the wave would do away with everything. Also, the army equipment and national guard vehicles needed to be moved. Before he finished his term, the governor of Puerto Rico finally moved everything.

FEMA has and keeps building storage facilities for all the supplies. Arrangements are being made to set up a new capital city in Puerto Rico for the aftermath of the event. They were thinking about Caguas, but we do not know if this is final. Whomever wants to say this is not so, be my guest. NASA tried to say it was not so and now look at them. They are in Puerto Rico stationed there at present, as they cannot leave by orders of the president. All will come to pass as Yahushua spoke regardless of who says it won't be so. Great anguish approaches the earth. The fulfillment of the beginning of sorrows talked about in Mathew 7:8 KJV is at hand. The beginning of sorrows brothers and sisters. We have been taking the message daily, even twice a day to this land of

Santo Domingo, to proclaim Yah's plans over Puerto Rico. Our voice is even hoarse from doing this. But you must understand that you have to prepare as well. because you will get the same here as we will get over there simultaneously."

SECTION FIVE

The Investigative Judgement of the Living Commences

The prophet speaks: - "The judgement will start at the hour of 2:00 AM in the morning. The president said that he did not want any more Puerto Ricans up there, so he decided to stock Puerto Rico up with all the benefits, so that nobody would move out of the island to the US. However, they are not obeying their mandate as leaders by keeping silent. The president has an underground shelter, ready for him, while everyone else would-be above suffering, and going through the worst tragedy. But above with us, will be the Lord looking after us. That is why He is coming in Person. He will not be on His throne that night, but with us to protect us. He will put His hand where the righteous are. Angels will be protecting us and our homes. It will be like the night of the execution of the first born in Egypt, when Father protected His people. That night, He will separate the church that truly serves Him from the one that does not serve Him. Most of the current church would die by execution that night, then new flocks will come in.

Many who are unbelievers will be its new leaders. It will be a new church; a new people; a new harvest because they believe more than the church nowadays does. Not only Puerto Rico but everywhere else. I pity the ones who keep believing that The Most High cannot and would not do this. He always warns the people who love Him, who honor Him truly, who know that He speaks, and that He lets His people know before bringing judgement. For love of His Son and His intersession, He warns us because we accept Him as our only and exclusive Savior: Yahushua HaMashiach, the Lord of Heaven is truly wonderful and beautiful. This nation is blessed. To those who open up their eyes to this, the Lord will protect you. To those who are watching this at home or wherever you are, this is not to instill fear. Please understand this. The Lord clearly told me, "The governor of Puerto Rico will leave the islands three days before My servant, he will abandon ship. He will leave the island." All leaders from the affected areas have been ordered to leave their territories beforehand. They will then return to their countries afterwards to see what remained of their people and their land. I simply tell you that The Father would not look the other way on whoever leader does this to his country. These leaders are under oath to protect their country of any situation internal or external, and The Most High would not ignore whether they keep their oath or not. He would honor the leaders who keep this oath and would protect them on that terrible day of judgement, that comes over Puerto Rico, Santo Domingo, and the United States.

The Lord has always sent signs of His judgement prior to executing it. He always, as a Father speaks to His flock; to His church; to His children beforehand. He does not leave them as orphans. He always honors His commitment to let them know, and he always activates His people, and

The Height of the Wave is Accurate as it Enters Las Marias and Maricao.

the warning given to them beforehand.

The height of the wave is accurate, as it enters Las Marias and Maricao. The Godhead would be on land to protect us from the powerful shock wave resulting from the asteroid impact. That huge wave would also be on its way to Santo Domingo that night. The details of the Lord's doing are not the same for every place, but the purpose is the same: to save people. You will tell Yahushua, "Let it not reach my home, and if it does, that the presence of the Holy Spirit covers us wherever we stand." If you are inside the house, maybe He would cover you with a protective air bubble or whatever He chooses.

If the earth is shaking by the twelve-point earthquake, may we not feel it in our homes, even if everything is trembling around you. You ask the

Lord for what you want. He will search your heart and will know if you serve Him or not. According to your lives the Lord will show mercy upon you. I know there will be plenty of miracles in all the Caribbean and the rest of the territories because The Most High will be defending many people who love Him. That is why the nuclear shock wave will not blow up our homes or do away with them. The Father's hand will be on earth protecting each and every one of His servants. The Holy Spirit and the angels will be supporting the columns of houses during the earthquake, so they do not crumble. The sea will pass by you or over you without touching you. Yah gives His guarantee to His true church; to the people who honor Him when they have much and when they have little. Those who choose the Lord over the world, because they tasted the world but prefer now to stay with the Lord, He will give you the opportunity to live, so you can testify to this. With all sincerity, make a new personal commitment to Him. Make changes in your life.

This wave will approach the island of Santo Domingo through the east, wreaking havoc. I

The Asteroid will Strike Mayaguez Puerto Rico, out in the Atlantic Ocean at 2:00 AM in the Morning.

assure you that the situation here will be worse than Puerto Rico. You have a larger population. The Most High guaranteed that there will be people who will remain alive in Puerto Rico. Many people will survive. The ones who serve the Him will help the wounded. We will speak to save the souls of those who are about to die without Ha Mashiach, and put their souls in His hands, making sure they confess the crucial words before dying. "I accept Yahushua Ha Mashiach as my only and exclusive Savior." Those are the most important words in our lives. This is why the Lord is telling the ones in this nation who have confessed those words about how the event would play out that night.

All that land in San Sabastian and Aguadilla in Puerto Rico are polluted; spiritually rotten. The church in that area mocked Yah. They will remain in that area that night to be executed. The Lord will gather the evil doers that night wherever they meet, together; those people who commit aberrant behavior, to be executed in their places of sin. He comes to cleanse the church and the land of many worldly sinners; witches, warlocks and satanic priest who do evil right now, not thinking twice about offending Him. In San Sabastian, there is a festival called the Festival of Den Ovilla. An ovilla is a cow. A Christian mayor together with the municipal assembly had the image of his cow erected to honor a satanic ritual in Puerto Rico called Fiestas Patronales which means Patron Saint Festivals, which are dedicated to saints and idols that offend The Most High. The statue was placed at the entrance of the municipality of San Sabastian. It does not look like a cow at all. It looks like a demon with the physical attributes of hell. The city hall of the nearby town of Aguadilla, also has a satanic image. The political leaders make covenants with the devil. They have been doing this for a long time. Politicians consult witches when it's election time. They consult them constantly.

Many Christians in the church practice witchcraft, looking after money, coveting abundance, prosperity. Secret satanic altars close to, or behind the actual altars of our Heavenly Father have been found. Pastors have been caught having double altars, praising Yahushua on one side and worshipping the devil on the other, entering secret rooms after the congregation have left, to worship the devil. This has been seen in Puerto Rico, and then they dare ask why such a judgement is coming. They polluted all that was holy, all the sacred vessels; everything. Just like in Daniel chapter five. We have been weighed like Belshazzar and have been found wanting. The finger of The Highest One of Israel has written on the wall about the continent, indicating that we have been found wanting, and judgement approaches. In this manner after the wave will be the manner in which He will cleanse this area with the sea, with salt water. He has shown this to unbelievers, to leaders of all kinds. If you only knew all the people who have called me, who have had Revelations about Puerto Rico, you would be amazed. The authorities are preparing for a cataclysmic event, even though they do not say the reason for the actual cataclysm. It would be something never before seen.

The tsunami waves will enter the cities at night. Many people who have had dreams about the waves, have seen similar images. It will enter Puerto Rico first at that magnitude. Puerto Rico is

The United States will be Hit After 5:00 AM. The Wave will enter Miami First.

the impact area, the epicenter of this judgement. The Father will be commanding the judgement from the land of Puerto Rico. That huge wave would reach the mountains that we showed before. He will cleanse the land. That is why I challenge the so-called servants of the Lord, those who say they fast and worship yet have no vision. You can do whatever, but if you have no presence of the Holy Spirit and the gift of discernment, or if you do not ask the Lord then you are wasting your time.

The Pharisees also fasted, and they knew the Word of the Most High inside and out, yet they were never ever able to understand His Son. They were blind. You will know if this is real or if this is a fallacy through the gift of discernment from the Holy Spirit. Thus said the Lord that this will be the impact. Those will be the two islands, yours Santo Domingo, and mine Puerto Rico where I was born; where I must remain and witness the event without running. That would be the exact point of impact. People from the US government, from the US army confirm that the point of impact will be there, but they confirmed this now, after seeing all the data from this

Arecibo Observatory Scientists Monitor for Expected Asteroid.

message. They say this under the table. Officially, they say nothing. Under the table they confirm that the impact will be as The Most High declared. His wrath would come down that night with fire and with that rock. His wrath will engulf the whole Caribbean area and would start a cleansing, beginning with the church of Ha Mashiach, to prepare it for the great rescue. This event of judgement will consummate the great harvest that has been announced about for so long.

The entire world will be in awe and in terror because of this situation, already announced and divulged by the Most High beforehand. So, the scientist of NASA gets no glory of any kind. Yah spoke about this first. Now they second this revelation, and as they said, "All that remains to do is pray." We would call on the Lord for His instructions for us. The church in this nation would not run. We will wait for the moment when He tells us to move to the safe places where we will be protected

Lot was protected in the mountains. I assure you that we will also go up to the mountains. Please do not do what was done here a few years ago. Someone predicted an earthquake and tsunami, and Christians fled to the mountains to wait. Nobody can predict an earthquake, nobody. Until today, nobody has been able to predict the exact time of an earthquake. We are not predicting exact times and dates of this judgement, but we are saying that it would be at night. We are also saying that there will be a specific sign for this event which I will tell you about soon. The Lord has a commitment to me as well as to you, to let us know of His plans. We can then ask Him, "What will you do about me then? What will you do with me, what about me. I am not up to your standards. I am at thirty percent." Speak like this to the Lord. You will ask Him in all sincerity, help me, help me be worthier. Take me to a higher percent of worthiness. I have always said that only Yahushua HaMashiah has the hundred percent. The Lord will add what we are lacking. Your sincerity when talking to Him will make the difference. It will make the difference on the mercy He will show you. That is why that night He will be walking on that island you see right there which looks like a lamb called Puerto Rico.

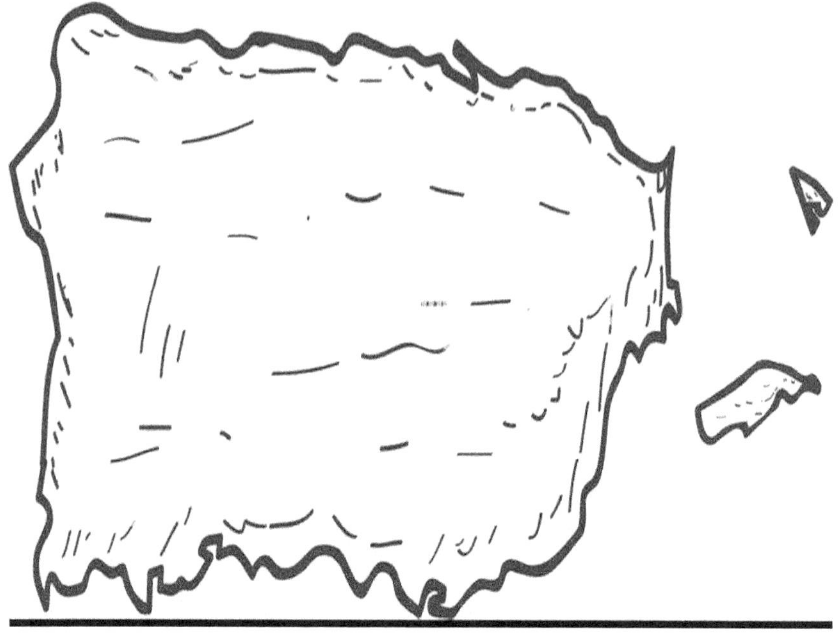

Puerto Rico's Land Mass is Shaped like a Lamb.

He has guaranteed that He would be on the ground to look after us. The Lord Yahushua will be claiming the souls of thousands upon thousands, who will depart with Him that night before the Father, who will also be watching the execution on land. That is why it is important for Him to be present during this judgement, which will be a partial judgement; yet complete in the sense that it will cleanse and prepare the new church. He will have absolute control of everything that happens. The sea will not go beyond where He has ordained it to go. It would not be a total destruction, but a judgement that will bring about change and cleansing for the church who will see our Lord's face.

The new continent, the new world is composed of lands that have been reached by the gospel basically in its entirety. The Lord has a commitment to the believers of this continent. He lets us know in advance so we can make the necessary changes and get ready with Him. We are doing the impossible to take this message to as many people as possible. Yesterday, we presented it to two congregations for over four hours each. We sometimes loose our voice in the process. We do it because of the importance and eminence of preparing the people. The photo indicates exactly how the judgement will come to pass. It will not happen in any other way. Our Father has absolute control over it. It will happen exactly as we have revealed it. I certify this in the name of Yahushua. NASA and the US government also certify this now. The high ranked military personnel in Puerto Rico are taking their families off the island. They haven't even seen this message. They have been called and told to leave the island while they can. Soon they won't be able to move anymore. What they don't know is that we have a supreme leader who looks after us. We have the Holy Spirit who will give us strength. He will protect us at the difficult moment. The army of the Lord will be gathering thousands, possibly millions of souls claimed by Him that night to depart with Him. The judgement will be at night because many here on this island and in Puerto Rico have prayed to the Lord to be together with their families in case of an earthquake or cataclysm. Not away from their children while they're in school, or while spouses and parents are away from each other. I tell you the land will keep trembling. There will continue to be earthquakes and other things, however, this judgement is one; unique! It is a total judgement for the church and the new flock, yet partial in terms of physical destruction. We will be with our families during the execution; all of us. We will do what we need to do because there is a sign of the fulfillment of this event. We will have a sign from the Father for the eminence of the event, and we must use this sign to prepare spiritually first. The Lord says in this word that when we see the fig tree blossom to lift up our heads. The fig tree is Israel which is now a nation. Since 1948 it has been a nation and a sign that the times of the book of Revelation are near. It is a sign for the church of Ha Mashiach to know He is near at the door. We also have a sign to be fulfilled for this judgement, previous to the events in the book of Revelation, to get the church ready for the great rescue which we will be a part of.

Those of us who remain alive after this chastisement will go all over the world to take this message to the rest of the countries of the world, which will be in total bewilderment. Countries that nowadays do not allow the preaching of the gospel. However, this message of prophecy already is being spread to these countries, that is why all the details of the prophecy has to be precise. Nothing will happen in a different manner than what is written. That is why when I take this message I do not fear, since the presence of the Godhead; the presence of the Holy Spirit goes with me. Therefore, I am not afraid to present it to the witches, the president, the satanists, whomever. Thus said the Lord, and thus would it come to pass as He declared. It's not a matter of being braver than anyone else. I told the US officials," Arrest me whenever you want, but I will not stop taking this message, not to create a panic, but so that the church everywhere prepares for the Lord. They wanted all this to be silenced, but we followed the instructions and prudence of our supreme leader; our Lord Yahushua HaMashiach.

We will go forth afterwards to help with the great rescue. Ezekiel 12 KJV clearly says that some will be allowed to escape, to tell about the abominations committed in the land, to testify before other nations. We will tell the Russians, "I was there at the moment of impact, and the Most High put forth His hand and protected me from the nuclear shock wave. He protected my house from the earthquake. I was living in the coastal area, and the sea passed over me without touching me. My Savior did that." We will bear witness and powerful testimonies from here and from there. We will tell them, "The true Holy One spoke first." This is why the gospel will enter many nations, all of them in this case. This will be the pre-amble of the beginning of sorrows and the great harvest that will prepare the church for the true rapture of the church. Right now, there will not be a rapture before this event. The rapture

A two-hundred-foot wave would sweep most of the North Coast of Puerto Rico.

will take place after this chastisement: after Yah has prepared a new flock that will enter in from every part of the world. We will then get ready to see our Lord Yahushua in the rapture. This event is meant to save multitudes, and to straighten up the church. That's why I said to those who are enjoying these new laws in Puerto Rico and in the US, that go against the mandates of God, "Enjoy them while you can. You think you have victory. You think you have won, but the war is won by the Father and by Yahushua."

This prophet lives in the municipality of Mateo in Puerto Rico. The wave entering the north area of the island would also approach his house.

The prophet speaks: - "My house has been paid off for almost eight to nine years, before the Lord affected my health so that I would give His message. The Lord knew I had financial and family obligations, and He did not want me to worry. That is why He allowed me to pay all my debts, so that no one could take away my house from my kids. He knows that I worry about my family. He knows that I worry about my obligations. I live in that area shown there, a beautiful place in a beautiful area of the north coast of Puerto Rico. I simply told the Lord, "What we own is yours." I have to abandon that place on that night of judgement because of what's coming. He took me and my family to the place where we will be during the judgement. I only ask the Lord to allow me to go back to my home after the event. Although He showed me that all the area would be swept away, all those homes will be gone, nevertheless, I told Him, "If it is your will, please let my house stand. Let me see it standing when I return, and please let it not get wet inside either." Because I think I am sincere with the Lord as to what He shows me. But I said, "Let it be your will." I simply asked. He will know if He will honor my request or not. I will do everything I can so that He also looks after you and honors you wherever you are.

FEMA is preparing for this in an urgent and quick manner. In a very very urgent hurried manner, they are preparing. That is what we are going to be facing in the north area of Puerto Rico that night. It would be a two-hundred-foot wave which would sweep most of the North Coast of Puerto

Rico. Those two hundred feet are exactly as The Most High dictated. The island would not be destroyed. The judgement would be as He dictated throughout the whole area. FEMA is preparing the northern municipalities such as Maimón, saying that the sea would reach up to the mountain area.

Our northern coast is very deep, that is why the wave would come in as the Lord said. The wave to hit the whole northern coast would be two hundred feet high. In Japan the highest wave was one hundred and thirty-eight feet high. The one we will face in the northern area is two hundred feet high. The one facing the western part of the island, where the impact will occur will be a thousand feet high. All is programmed by the Lord so that it occurs as He dictated. That is why He told me to bring the message with all details and photos to the people. He told me, "My servant, my people will not believe. All I want is for them not to have excuses before me." Here, over there and wherever we go, because just like in Israel the people mocked the Word of The Lord spoken through His prophets, but the chastisement always fell on them. Afterwards, He executed judgement, then they came to Him crying, wailing wounded. The people are being told beforehand of His plans. All areas will be controlled by the Lord of Heaven within the judgement. You will ask Him what will happen here on this island of Santo Domingo. I will simply tell you what I told the pastors in Puerto Rico. The Lord asked me, "My servant, my servant, do you remember Korah?" He asked me this five times. When I finally nodded, it was midnight, then He told me, "My servant, that is what I will do to the majority of pastors in Puerto Rico, they will go alive to Hell when I open up the earth beneath them. They have mocked the Lord, they have thrown away His postulates, they have not warned the people. They have toyed with the Word. "I will open up the earth during the earthquake wherever they are, and they will go to Hell alive that night. There will be witnesses."

There is a remnant of pastors in Puerto Rico who have been true to the gospel and who will be protected by Yah. The Lord told me, "The substitutes of these pastors are already seated within their churches. The flocks that remain alive my servant, will go with these new leaders that I will lift up. A great harvest comes to Puerto Rico and Santo Domingo. The same will happen here on this island of Santo Domingo. Those of you who have scores to settle with the Lord, get to it already, before He demands an account of whatever you need to fix. This is no joke. It is very serious. I have challenged the pastors in Puerto Rico to prove me untruthful through the presence of the Holy Spirit. None have done so. They are mute because the Holy Spirit will not refute my words. I come on His behalf."

The Sign for this Catastrophic Judgement

The prophet speaks: - "There is a sign for the church of Yahushua. The sign is the person you see on the message. It's a special message to brother G J Avila. He chose this man as a sign for the church to prepare for the coming judgement. This man has unmatched credentials before Him and before men, as an evangelist and servant of the Lord through and through. This man departing with the Lord is the sign appointed for me and for His whole church. Nobody can cast a stone at him. Nobody can point at him spiritually; he served the Lord in plenty and in need. He did things that no one else has done. He served the Lord and was tested. Tested in a way that I myself cannot say that I could have withstood. He has all the requisites for the Lord to single him out as the sign for His judgement. Many say why him? There are people in Puerto Rico and Santo Domingo who are also righteous, but his man has done things that none other have done. His credentials before the Lord are untouchable and before man too. I spoke to him in person for about forty minutes and let him know all about this message and about The Most High's choice of him as a sign for the judgement. I told him thus said Yah. I had told Yah that I would not deliver this message to the people, until I talked to G J Avila, gave him the message, and got his approval. I told the Lord, "If G J does not accept the message, I will not deliver it to the people no matter what you do to me." I talked to G J and told him all the details as Yah showed me. I told him that the Lord would take him before the rapture, not in the rapture as he had stated publicly. The Most High sent word that He would take him before the rapture.

"There will be a judgement executed over Puerto Rico, but you will not see it," I told him. G J has pure presence of the Lord. Nobody can come to him with a message like this one without having the Holy Spirit as the one who speaks it. I was talking to a man used by Father like no other. The Most High could reveal to him whether this was from Him or not. The Lord sent me, however, to give him the details. I told him everything…….. After I finished talking, I stood up and told him that I was leaving. "I will see you in Heaven," I told him. He stood up and told me, "Don't go, I will pray for you." I said, "Amen." He said, "But first, I will ask something of you." At that point I got nervous because I thought he was going to reject the message, but he simply told me, "All that you have just told me go quickly and tell it to the people, do not omit a word." He told me this a second and a third time with emphasis. I said, "That's what I'll do."

From that moment on I have not rested. Day and night I have taken the message, tired exhausted and losing my hair. Look how my hair is going. There is a lot of worry involved. But I prefer to lose my hair than to lose my soul to Hell. I'll take this message anywhere; anywhere He sends me, no matter what the cost. The Lord told me, "My servant, as soon as the remains of my servant G J are laid to rest, I will send the judgement over Puerto Rico and the Caribbean." But He said, "Before that, I will allow the people to honor him." Currently, an arena is being reserved for that event as soon as he departs with the Lord. Nobody is killing him here. When the Lord takes him, we will know if the Lord spoke or not. G J will be the sign.

According to Yah, the judgement will happen at night. G J will be buried during the day. Whether the judgement comes the first day or the next day after G J's burial or whenever, I do not know. All I know is that I will be asking the Holy Spirit constantly, "Tell me when do I leave, when do I move?" You will receive prior warning that night from angels of the Lord, knocking on your doors, and the Lord with His angels will tell you, "My servant, move to such and such a place, or my servant, stay inside your home." The Lord will tell each person differently. He will let His people know because it is Him who gives notice. The time is 2:00 AM in the morning. The day, however, would be a day chosen by the Lord only after the death of G J Avila. G J will take with him some secrets I told him in person which I cannot reveal. Regardless of any faults that anyone may find in him, he is the sign chosen by The Most High for this judgement, like He used Moses's staff as the sign of His power. This man G J, even after death, will be the sign for multitudes to be saved. We are not idolaters. We do not idolize men, but the Godhead is honoring him because he has all the credentials before Yah of a true believer and servant of the Lord. That is why Yah chose him. Currently, this man's health is very fragile, and he is bedridden. We are only waiting for the moment when the Lord of Heaven will decide to take this servant into His presence. This is what is currently going on in Puerto Rico. We are waiting. Meanwhile the Lord sent us urgently to this nation to declare to you how this judgement will take place.

A pastor from the United States came several years ago saying that the world would end on May 25th. When we saw that we thought, "What madness, a pastor saying this." We knew beforehand of course that the world would not end: however, they opened up all sorts of media to broadcast his message. Open the doors to this message too, and you would soon know if The Most High spoke through it or if it was just a man. You would see it with your own eyes, I guarantee it. There is no turning back. Yahushua is calling the ones who have gone astray to run, not from terror to escape, but to run to His feet for protection, for them and for their families. Those who are sinning within the church, get right with the Lord.

Pastors, you need the Holy Spirit to come back to your churches. You need to reclaim that presence. Get the dancers out, and all fleshly things out of the temples and churches. Stop telling people that everything will be abundant. We will experience lack. We will experience need soon, but the Father will provide within it to His flock, to His people. He is committed to us through His Son, to provide for us under all circumstances. That is why we declare this message in detail. There is further information, but it is too much to declare here. Any of you who wish to do so may call me on 787-244-5434, and I will send you all the written information from different sources, indicating that this disaster approaches, yet the Lord will have absolute control of it. My email address is efraimrodriguez556@yahoo.com. The United States has not put me in jail because they know that the message already travels the world and would only give strength to the alert.

The church is called to let the people know without creating panic. Please do not create a panic. Prepare and store food and water. We will be waiting for instructions from the Lord. In this nation, if you do like we are all called to do, you will be protected. Pray, asking Father to send angels to save you like He did with Peter. Also pray for the advocates of Heaven to speak the truth. Believe me, we are not in fear. We are not the most brave but we have the reassurance that the one who sent us would defend us in any situation. That is why we have taken this difficult message to Puerto Rico and the US. All that remains for the government to do is to come clean and declare the truth, at least so that people can prepare. They no longer would get any glory or credit because the Lord spoke first. We trust that He will protect us in the coming night;

in the minutes that remain before this judgement. And we hope the church wakes up and reacts. The church needs to seriously start seeking the Lord. It needs to leave fornication behind, both fornication of the Word as physical fornication. It needs to stop adultery. It needs to stop the homosexuality in the temples and churches. There is a decree from the beginning. Man has violated this, but it is the decree of The Most High and will prevail until the end. Male and female they were created.

Homosexual men and women have called me to pray for them so that they can leave that kind of behavior behind. A young homosexual man called me and told me, "Brother, I do not practice it with others, but I like it and I don't know how to leave it behind." We prayed and he told me, "I feel better." We kept talking later on, and he said that he really wanted to change. A young woman with the same problem also asked me, "What must I do. I need to get out of this, I need to leave this." So many people have called me in the same manner, you have no idea. People within the church who are oppressed, because when the message comes from The Lord, the Holy Spirit convicts them. They make the change because they recognize the need for that change, just like the drug addicts who want to leave their addiction behind but cannot. You need to rebuke these demons that keep you captive. You have to struggle to come back, like I did to be able to take this most difficult message to the whole continent. Santo Domingo will also have their night before The Lord, and I hope you understand that you have to run; not to another place, but to the feet of Yahushua HaMashiach.

The guarantee of Heaven will assure you as soon as you do this. The Holy Spirit will give you strength and you will not experience fear of any kind. The Holy Spirit guarantees security. I want you to understand that this is a very long message. What we have given you here is an excerpt of the most important points so you can be aware. Make urgent arrangements with your families. Make peace with your neighbors and everybody else. Stop speaking filthy words. I have noticed that believers here and in Puerto Rico speak improper words, and then they speak in tongues inside the church. We would have to see what kind of tongues they are actually speaking. I have to speak clearly and with rectitude so that the Holy Spirit uses us. All this evil runs a mock in our churches and temples. All the postulates of the Lord have been violated. That is why He would perform this judgement. It is irrevocable, no one can stop it.

The Most High loves this nation of Santo Domingo also. There are many believers here. There are also unbelievers whom He also loves, and that would be part of the beautiful blessing. We would see each other at a future time. Soon we would see if the Lord spoke. And most importantly, to all those who have viewed and heard this message, please analyze it, ask Him. Whether you serve Yahushua or not, He is willing and ready to hear you and to show you what you ask of Him, so you can return to Him, where there is a guarantee of salvation and protection.

Time is short. May the Lord bless you, keep you and open your heart to this warning in Yahushua HaMashiach's name. AMEN."

1. ***Scientist*** have indicated that this asteroid impact will stop the rotation of the earth for three days." [Pg 61]

As a writer, since these words were not spoken by Yahushua but by scientists, I therefore question the validity of this statement pertaining to the stopping of the rotation of earth. I have not seen any quote in the Bible that says the rotation of the earth will stop for three days, and that once this period is over, the Most High will begin rotating it again. What I have read is, "And he opened the bottomless pit; and there arose a smoke out of the pit, as the smoke of a great furnace; and the sun and the air were darkened by reason of the smoke of the pit," Revelation 9:2 KJV. This confirms the vision given on "U B Ready" channel which says,

2."This darkness will appear as thick black smoke or fog and will cover the entire earth. My son, this darkness come from man wanting to open portals into other dimensions, but instead, open the gates of hell to lose upon the world great evil." [Pg 21]

SECTION SIX

The Second Exodus

And after these events, the Lord will also bring the Hebrews out from Mystery Babylon (The United States of America) and around the rest of the world, just like He brought the children of Israel out from the land of Egypt, after the three days and nights of darkness, and the death of all the first born of Egypt. Exodus 12:31-33 KJV reads "Then Pharaoh called for Moses and Aaron at night. He said, Get up and go away from my people, both you and the people of Israel. Go and worship the Lord, as you have said. take your flocks and your cattle, as you have said, and go. And pray that good will come to me also. The Egyptians were trying to make the people hurry out of the land. For they said, "We will all be dead."

In like manner, after all the deaths resulting from the earthquake, tsunami and three days and nights of darkness, the house of Jacob along with some

Royal Caribbean's Icon of the Seas: The World's Largest Cruise Ship Will Set Sail In 2024.

gentiles will also board ships to leave this place and around the world to go and serve The Most High in the wilderness. The Highest one of Israel will then no longer visit those people, who for one reason or the other did not leave Mystery Babylon and the countries under her umbrella for their redemption, but only in judgement. Here in Amos 8 KJV, The Most High speaks to the House of Jacob: His own people, and not to the other nations saying, "Thus hath the Lord GOD shewed unto me: and behold a basket of summer fruit.

This represents the Harvested People of Israel.

And he said, Amos, what seest thou? And I said, A basket of summer fruit. Then said the LORD unto me, The end is come upon my people of Israel; I will not again pass by them any more." Amos 8:1,2 KJV. fruit

1. The purpose of this vision was to show that the people were ripe for judgment, that God's forbearance was at an end. The divine long-suffering had resulted only in the continuance of Israel's sin."

Therefore, what's left but for the Most High to judge, abandon and cut off the unrepentant as in Amos 8:1,2 KJV. This represents the Harvested People of Israel, as Yahuveh never again return to the unrepentant. And for many the cry will be heard, "The harvest is past, the summer is ended, and we are not saved," Jeremiah 8:20 KJV.

A Message to the Hebrews and Gentile Nations from Yahuveh

This can be found on the You Tube channel "Disciples of Yah."

"Tell my children that a great wave of darkness is coming to cover the earth unlike since the beginning of time. Tell them Ha-Satan and his

The SDA Bible Commentary, vol. 4, p. 979.[1]

minions are approaching; three days of darkness. They, Ha-Satan will walk the earth. Any human found outside during this time will be killed by them. Many souls will perish my son for ignorance and disobedience for not following my words. Tell your families or else their blood will be on your hands. Even though they don't listen. Remember obedience is better than sacrifice. For you are children of truth and must walk and speak truth. These days will seem scary, but I will be with you. Powers to be unlocked. Dominion to reclaim after the darkness. Walk and leave the land with great wealth and regather to a central location. My angels and leaders will guide the way to the wilderness. Many will come, but many will be left behind. When gifts are activated, begin to walk in them, no gifts to lie dormant. Time is short, we move like lightning. Things will start to look like a flash but it's me removing my people from the lands of their captivity. Ha-Satan will be on our trail on our way out, but you all will be protected. My angels will fight and deal with the devourer, so will my hundred forty-four thousand (144000.) Tell my people, final messages and plans are about to go into effect. Get in place, be ready, we move like lightning. Remember, you are light. You are electric. Roar like a lion with the voices of thunder and move like lightning my children. Yahuveh Sabaoth has spoken. Any man or woman who deny the words of my prophet or prophetess; my Son would deny on the day of judgement."

During these three days and nights of darkness, some of the minions working with Ha-Satan will include that which is spoken of in the following verses of Revelation 9:13-16 KJV which reads, "And the sixth angel sounded, and I heard a voice from the four horns of the golden altar which is before God, Saying to the sixth angel which had the trumpet, Loose the four angels which are bound in the great river Euphrates. And the four angels were loosed, which were prepared for an hour, and a day, and a month, and a year, for to slay the third part of men." Angels are very powerful beings. Just look at what one angel did to the Assyrian army. "And it came to pass that night, that the angel of the LORD went out, and smote in the camp of the Assyrians an hundred fourscore and five thousand: and when they arose early in the morning, behold, they *were* all dead corpses." 2 Kings 19:35 KJV. Now consider this; if one good angel could singlehandedly kill so many solders in one instance, how much more would angry evil "angels which kept not their first estate, but left their own habitation, he hath reserved in everlasting chains under darkness unto the judgment of the great day," Jude 6 KJV. Just released from their chains under the Great River Euphrates, finally let loose and extremely angry for having beings pent up in darkness for so long, now finally set free, and ready to tear up anyone who gets in their way. The third part of men is not a small number. Plus, there will also be minions of other fallen angels and demons roaming around during the dark period. This is not a pretty picture. Satan does his best work in the dark.

The above-mentioned messenger has also noted that we cannot bring huge amounts of our belongings but will only be allowed to carry maybe a suitcase and a duffle bag with our valuables, together with a little food and water. He also said that it is necessary to consult the Holy Spirit on this, since every situation will be different. Most importantly is that no electronics will be permitted on this journey. All electronics

must stay here in Mystery Babylon (America).

The Different Modes of Transport to get to the Wilderness.

From a more present-day perspective, let us continue to look at not only when, but also how this exodus will take place. Unlike the first one where the Hebrew Israelites walked out of Egypt, there will be several means of transportation provided to get people to the wilderness; the first of which is by sea. These cruise ships, otherwise known as Freedom ships (Free from Edom ships) are called the ships of Tarshish. The scripture that pertains reads, "Who *are* these *that* fly as a cloud,

and as the doves to their windows?

Surely the isles shall wait for me, and the ships of Tarshish first, to bring thy sons from far, their

silver and their gold with them, unto the name of the LORD thy God, and to the Holy One of Israel, because he hath glorified thee." Isaiah 60:8,9 KJV And I will set a sign [the 144000] among them, and I will send those that escape of them [after the catastrophic initial judgment of the living] unto the nations, to Tarshish, Pul, and Lud, that draw the bow, to Tubal, and Javan, to the isles afar off, that have not heard my fame, neither have seen my glory; and they shall declare my glory among the Gentiles. And they shall bring all your brethren [the great multitude] for an offering unto the Lord out of all nations upon horses,

and in chariots,

and in litters,

and upon mules,

and upon swift beasts,

to my holy mountain Jerusalem, saith the Lord, as the children of Israel bring an offering in a clean vessel into the house of the Lord. And I will also take of them for priests and for Levites,

saith the Lord. Isaiah 66:19-21 KJV.

The Wilderness: A Place Prepared by Yahuveh

All things have been prepared and are now ready in the wilderness to accommodate you. There is therefore absolutely no reason to remain here in Mystery Babylon (America) or in any other country that would be affected by the Mark of the Beast decree, under the rule of anti-christ Nimrod.

Some of the children will be rescued by angels before the judgement begins, Jeremiah 31;15 KJV. It is called the rescue of the innocent. But, since we don't know exactly whom the Most High would take, pack for your children as well. Don't take any chances. Flee Babylon when the sun returns after the three days and nights of darkness! "Come out of her my people that ye be not partakers of her sins and that ye receive not of her plagues," Revelation 18:4 KJV. Flee to the wilderness! Revelation 12: 6,14 KJV reads, "And the woman fled into the wilderness, where she hath a place prepared of God, that they should feed her there a thousand two hundred and threescore days. And to the woman were given

Earthquakes, Floods, Volcanoes, Sinkholes: Fury Poured out.

Tsunamis, Tornadoes, Fires, Ice Storms: Fury Poured Out.

two wings of a great eagle, that she might fly into the wilderness, into her place, where she is nourished for a time, and times, and half a time (3 1/2 years: 42 months), from the face of the serpent."

For "As I live, saith the Lord GOD, surely with a mighty hand, and with a stretched out arm, and with fury poured out, will I rule over you: And I will bring you out from the people, and will gather you out of the countries wherein ye are scattered, with a mighty hand, and with a stretched out arm, and with fury poured out. And I will bring you into the wilderness of the people, and there will I plead with you face to face. Like as I pleaded with your fathers in the wilderness of the land of Egypt, so will I plead with you, saith the Lord GOD, And I will cause you to pass under the rod, and I will bring you into the bond of the covenant: And I will purge out from among you the rebels, and them that transgress against me: I will bring them forth out of the country where they sojourn, and they shall not enter into the land of Israel: and ye shall know that I am the LORD," Ezekiel 20:33-38 KJV. "Therefore say, Thus saith the Lord GOD; I will even gather you

147

from the people, and assemble you out of the countries where ye have been scattered, and I will give you the land of Israel," Ezekiel 11:17 KJV.

If The Most High has prepared Heaven, earth, and the entire universe, then it is not difficult for Him to prepare the wilderness beautifully for His people: the Israelites.

We are Israelites not Israelis.

We are not Israelis, we are Israelites

"O Lord our God, thou hast dealt with us after all thy goodness, and according to all that great mercy of thine, As thou spakest by thy servant Moses in the day when thou didst command him to write the law before the children of Israel, saying, If ye will not hear my voice, surely this very great multitude shall be turned into a small number among the nations, where I will scatter them. For I knew that they would not hear me, because it is a stiffnecked people: but in the land of their captivities they shall remember themselves. And shall know that I am the Lord their God: for I will give them an heart, and ears to hear: And they shall praise me in the land of their captivity, and think upon my name, And return from their stiff neck, and from their wicked deeds: for they shall remember the way of their fathers, which sinned before the Lord." Baruch 2:27-33 KJV

We are not Israelis, we are Israelites. Therefore, trust The Most High Yah and flee Babylon! We are the people of the Book. Isaiah 60:1-7 KJV reads, "Arise, shine; for thy light is come, and the glory of the LORD is risen upon thee. For, behold, the darkness shall cover the earth, and gross darkness the people: but the LORD shall arise upon thee, and his glory shall be seen upon thee. And the Gentiles shall come to thy light, and kings to the brightness of thy rising.

Modern Day Monarchy

Lift up thine eyes round about, and see: all they gather themselves together, they come to thee: thy sons shall come from far, and thy daughters shall be nursed at thy side. Then thou shalt see, and flow together, and thine heart shall fear, and be enlarged; because the abundance of the sea shall be converted unto thee, the forces of the

Gentiles shall come unto thee. The multitude of camels shall cover thee, the dromedaries of Midian and Ephah; all they from Sheba shall come: they shall bring gold and incense; and they shall shew forth the praises of the LORD. All the flocks of Kedar shall be gathered together unto thee, the rams of Nebaioth shall minister unto

Gold and Incense

thee: they shall come up with acceptance on mine altar, and I will glorify the house of my glory." All these riches belong to and are ready for us.

Repentance is Key

When Yahuveh sent Jonah to Nineveh of Assyria with the message of repentance, they immediately got down in sackcloth and ashes and repented, and as a result, He spared Nineveh.

151

They were not destroyed. Jonah 3:5-10 KJV reads, "So the people of Nineveh believed God, and proclaimed a fast, and put on sackcloth, from the greatest of them even to the least of them. For word came unto the king of Nineveh, and he arose from his throne, and he laid his robe from him, and covered him with sackcloth, and sat

The Repentance of Nineveh

in ashes. And he caused it to be proclaimed and published through Nineveh by the decree of the king and his nobles, saying, Let neither man nor beast, herd nor flock, taste any thing: let them not feed, nor drink water: But let man and beast be covered with sackcloth, and cry mightily unto God: yea, let them turn every one from his evil way, and from the violence that is in their hands. Who can tell if God will turn and repent, and turn away from his fierce anger, that we perish not? And God saw their works, that they turned from their evil way; and God repented of the evil, that he had said that he would do unto them; and he did it not."

Today the Most High is asking the entire world to repent, including the leaders of each individual country. The coming judgements will affect every nation on this planet, it will be severe. "And the slain of the LORD shall be at that day from one

Fire and Sword of War

153

end of the earth even unto the other end of the earth: they shall not be lamented, neither gathered, nor buried; they shall be dung upon the ground," Jeremiah 25:33 KJV. "For by fire and by his sword will the LORD plead with all flesh: and the slain of the LORD shall be many," Isaiah 66:16 KJV.

But if the leaders of your countries refuse to do what Nineveh did, to call that country under their leadership to repent and lead that repentance, then you must do so individually. "Seek ye the LORD, all ye meek of the earth, which have wrought his judgment; seek righteousness, seek meekness: it may be ye shall be hid in the day of the LORD'S anger." Zephaniah 2:3 KJV.

So, to all those who are reading this discourse, I would say, humble yourself before the Most High. Confess your sins, repent, and make your restitution. Confession is your passport out of here. Restitution is your visa and repentance is your free ticket out of here. This is all you need to do to make it through these coming events and the Second Exodus, as you continue to walk in holiness, and He will lift you up.

CONCLUSION

The emphasis of this exposition is mainly on the three days and nights of darkness. Listen to what The Most-High, through His disciple Stephen Peterson said to explain this phenomenon.

Disciple Stephen Peterson

He said, "Many people will think that the three days of darkness is a solar eclipse because my people suffer for a lack of knowledge, Hosea 4:6 KJV. Those three days are fastly approaching. Don't get caught like a thief in the night. I sent this darkness. It was the casting out of the dragon in Heaven in Revelation 12 KJV. When cast into the earth, He would roam seeking whom he may devour for three days and nights. Just as Yahushua conquered death, so shall anyone not caught in darkness outside will as well. Many call it the death angel which is true. But I am the God of truth, and my Son is the ruler of life. Ha Satan is the ruler of all darkness. He is the king of death. He is and will be killing all who are not in their dwelling with my hands of protection. My one forty-four, they would astro project (spiritually) and would go onto Mt Zion and meet with Yahushua for instructions. This is the revelation of the concealed word of the three days of darkness. Believe in the words of my prophet. Read Revelation 12:3-7, 9 KJV."

Then the Holy Spirit revealed that the biggest deception took place in 1948 with the Jewish people, how they were supposed to be the people of the land. They managed to fool the whole world including us Israelites before we became awakened. The second biggest deception was the Covid-19 and its vaccine. From 1948 to now 2023 has been seventy-five years. Seventy-five distinguishes and means to enter into contention and to fight with the adversary who in this case is Ha Satan. Psalm 75 elaborates on this with particular emphasis on verse ten which says, "**All** the horns of the wicked also will I cut off; but the horns of the righteous shall be exalted." Daniel 12: 4 KJV reads, "But thou, O Daniel, shut up the words, and seal the book, *even* to the time of the end: many shall run to and fro, and knowledge shall be increased." This is knowledge increased brought to us from the Highest through a disciple of His choice. It is time for the wicked to drink of the cup wrung out with Yahuveh's wrath unto them in judgment. The gentiles will now be demoted while the real Israel will be exalted. This is a declaration of Yahuveh's resolution of executing judgment. He is removing the church of Philadelphia to "keep thee from the hour of temptation, which shall come upon all the world, to try them that dwell upon the earth," Revelation 7:10 KJV, for only under His wings will we find divine protection; then the Second Exodus commences. But if you decide that you won't leave, when all fossil fuel is discontinued, you will sit down in darkness with no light. You will sit down in the cold with no heat. You will sit down in the heat with no air conditioning. You will sit down in hunger with no food.

Absolutely no electronics or pets are allowed to be taken with us at Yahuveh's command. Therefore, please be obedient and follow all

All such items will be confiscated before leaving the ports.

His instructions. It is imperative for our

protection during this time. For thus saith the WORD, "When thy judgments are in the earth, the inhabitants of the world will learn righteousness," Isaiah 26:9 KJV.

Warning

Events pointing to, surrounding and involving the Three Days and Nights of Darkness must not be taken lightly.

O Flat Earth

In Isaiah 24:1-4 KJV, Most High says to the **world**, "Behold, the LORD maketh the earth empty, and maketh it waste, and turneth it upside down, and scattereth abroad the inhabitants thereof. And it shall be, as with the people, so with the priest; as with the servant, so with his master; as with the maid, so with her mistress; as with the buyer, so with the seller; as with the lender, so with the borrower; as with the taker of usury, so with the giver of usury to him. The land shall be utterly emptied, and utterly spoiled: for the LORD hath spoken this word. The earth mourneth and fadeth away, the world languisheth and fadeth away, the haughty people of the earth do languish.

Land Map of the USA

To the **United States of America**, Yahushua HaMashiach says, "Your country is desolate, your cities are burned with fire: your land, strangers devour it in your presence, and it is desolate, as overthrown by strangers," Isaiah 1:7 KJV. This kick-off event of invasion and fiery attacks takes place before Revelation 6 KJV, describing a great earthquake with tsunami, and also the darkness to come. The land is invaded and will soon be

159

attacked by foreign forces, making things more complicated as the darkness falls. "Come down,

Foreign Forces Invade America

and sit in the dust, O virgin daughter of Babylon, sit on the ground: *there is* no throne, O daughter of the Chaldeans (USA): for thou shalt no more be called tender and delicate," Isaiah 47:1 KJV.

Behold, a day is coming!

"Sit thou silent, and get thee into darkness, O daughter of the Chaldeans: for thou shalt no more be called, The lady of kingdoms," Isaiah 47:5 KJV.

The lady with her torch represents Lucifer the light bearer. "Behold, a day is coming for the LORD, when the spoil taken from you will be divided in your midst," Zechariah 14:1 KJV.

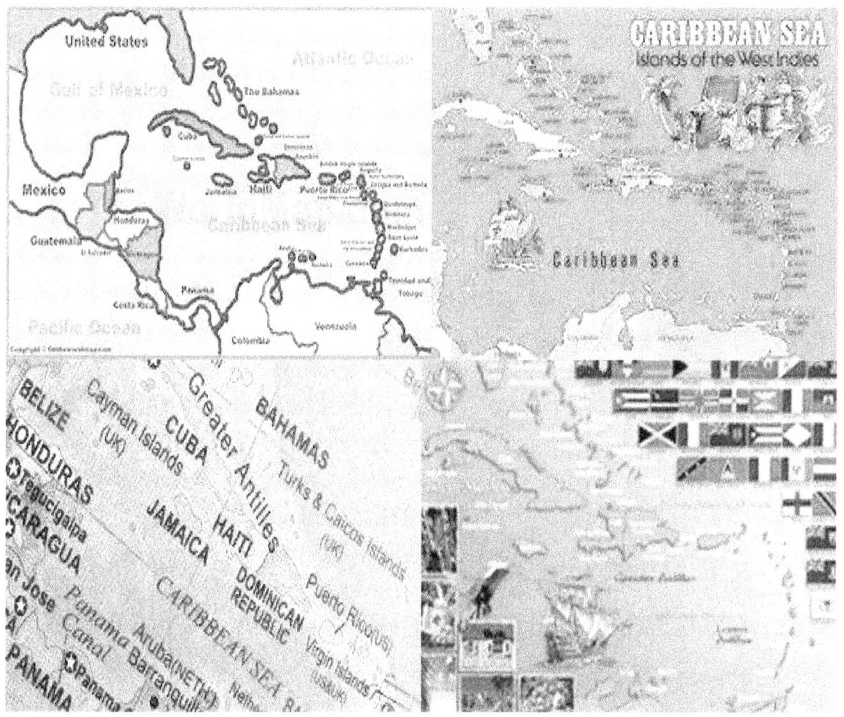

Tropical Islands of the Caribbean

To the **Caribbean** islands the Highest says, "And the great city (America) was divided into three parts, and the cities of the nations fell: and great Babylon (USA) came in remembrance before God, to give unto her the cup of the wine of the fierceness of his wrath. And every island fled away, and the mountains were not found."

161

Therefore, after the asteroid hit, resulting in a twelve point earthquake on the Richter magnitude scale, what can be expected here in America are three affected fault lines, two of which most of us are well aware of, namely the San Andres Fault in California, and the New Madrid Fault in the northern part of Mississippi embayment, along with the less talked about Cascadian Subduction Zone off the coast of the Pacific Northwest. But the Caribbean islands will also be affected, as Revelation 6:14 KJV makes this very clear stating that, "the heaven departed as a scroll when it is rolled together; and every mountain and island were moved out of their places." These islands are surrounded by the ocean, hence, once they move out of their place, there is nowhere else for them to go but to be buried in the deep blue sea.

Great judgements will continue to fall followed by death. "Behold a pale horse: and his name that sat on him was Death, and Hell followed with him. And power was given unto them over the fourth part of the earth, to kill with sword, and with hunger, and with death, and with the beasts of the earth, Revelation 6:8 KJV. Here we see that the aftermath of judgement will also cause death, but based on 2 Corinthians 5:8 KJV, "To be absent from the body, is to be present with the Lord." having a blessed assurance that, "Precious in the sight of the LORD *is* the death of his saints," Psalms 116:15 KJV.

On a worldwide scale, no one will escape what is to come, but what we can do is to PREPARE for it. Repentance is the free ticket out of here with final destination to the Kingdom of Yahuveh. Psalm 51 KJV is recommended for this process. Repeat it in sincerity and ask Yahushua HaMashiach for forgiveness of all sins known and unknown, and to have mercy. When confessing, each sin must be named one by one individually. Yahushua is merciful, "longsuffering to us-ward, not willing that any should perish, but that all should come to repentance," 2 Peter:3:9 KJV.

Psalm 51

[1]Have mercy upon me, O God, according to thy lovingkindness: according unto the multitude of thy tender mercies blot out my transgressions. [2]Wash me throughly from mine iniquity, and cleanse me from my sin.

³ For I acknowledge my transgressions: and my sin is ever before me.

⁴ Against thee, thee only, have I sinned, and done this evil in thy sight: that thou mightest be justified when thou speakest, and be clear when thou judgest.

⁵ Behold, I was shapen in iniquity; and in sin did my mother conceive me.

⁶ Behold, thou desirest truth in the inward parts: and in the hidden part thou shalt make me to know wisdom.

⁷ Purge me with hyssop, and I shall be clean: wash me, and I shall be whiter than snow.

⁸ Make me to hear joy and gladness; that the bones which thou hast broken may rejoice.

⁹ Hide thy face from my sins, and blot out all mine iniquities.

¹⁰ Create in me a clean heart, O God; and renew a right spirit within me.

¹¹ Cast me not away from thy presence; and take not thy holy spirit from me.

¹² Restore unto me the joy of thy salvation; and uphold me with thy free spirit.

¹³ Then will I teach transgressors thy ways; and sinners shall be converted unto thee.

¹⁴ Deliver me from bloodguiltiness, O God, thou God of my salvation: and my tongue shall sing

aloud of thy righteousness.

¹⁵ O Lord, open thou my lips; and my mouth shall shew forth thy praise.

¹⁶ For thou desirest not sacrifice; else would I give it: thou delightest not in burnt offering.

¹⁷ The sacrifices of God are a broken spirit: a broken and a contrite heart, O God, thou wilt not despise.

¹⁸ Do good in thy good pleasure unto Zion: build thou the walls of Jerusalem.

¹⁹ Then shalt thou be pleased with the sacrifices of righteousness, with burnt offering and whole burnt offering: then shall they offer bullocks upon thine altar.

Admonition

Fear no evil, what will be will be. It will get a whole lot worse before it gets better, but Most High, His Son and the Holy Spirit are always with us. Angels from under the Euphrates will be released, Revelation 9:15 KJV. The devil and his angels will be cast out of the second heaven into the earth, Revelation 12:9 KJV. So put your trust in Yahushua and believe in what He has said which is, "And, lo, I am with you alway, even unto the end of the world. Amen, Mathew 28:20 KJV.

Psalm 91: Divine Protection

[1] He that dwelleth in the secret place of the most High shall abide under the shadow of the Almighty.

[2] I will say of the LORD, He is my refuge and my fortress: my God; in him will I trust.

[3] Surely he shall deliver thee from the snare of the fowler, and from the noisome pestilence.

[4] He shall cover thee with his feathers, and under his wings shalt thou trust: his truth shall be thy shield and buckler.

[5] Thou shalt not be afraid for the terror by night; nor for the arrow that flieth by day;
[6] Nor for the pestilence that walketh in darkness;

⁶ Nor for the pestilence that walketh in darkness; nor for the destruction that wasteth at noonday.

⁷ A thousand shall fall at thy side, and ten thousand at thy right hand; but it shall not come nigh thee.

⁸ Only with thine eyes shalt thou behold and see the reward of the wicked.

⁹ Because thou hast made the LORD, which is my refuge, even the Most High, thy habitation;

¹⁰ There shall no evil befall thee, neither shall any plague come nigh thy dwelling.

¹¹ For he shall give his angels charge over thee, to keep thee in all thy ways.

¹² They shall bear thee up in their hands, lest thou dash thy foot against a stone.

¹³ Thou shalt tread upon the lion and adder: the young lion and the dragon shalt thou trample under feet.

¹⁴ Because he hath set his love upon me, therefore will I deliver him: I will set him on high, because he hath known my name.

[15] He shall call upon me, and I will answer him: I will be with him in trouble; I will deliver him, and honour him.

[16] With long life will I satisfy him, and shew him my salvation.

O World in Darkness

72 Hours

Gross

Darkness

Prepare!

Index

A

B

C

 173

Lamb 107
Las Marías and Maricao 82,97
Levite 143
Lightening 134
Litters 140
Lud 137
Lukewarm 8

M

Macaiah 87
Maimón 115
Marriage Supper 30
Medical Doctors 77
Midian 151
Million 87
Missiles 92
Moses 2
Most High 13
Mules 141
Mystery Babylon 37,46,129

N

NASA 109
Nazarene 31
Nebaioth 151
New Jerusalem 31
Nimrod 34
Nineveh 59,85,151
Noah 64
Non-transparent Fog 26
Northern Lights, 18, 27

O

Observatory 49

 176

World 158
Wrath 37

X

Y
Yahushua HaMashiach 13
Yahuveh 54

Z
Zion 30